CRUSADE AT THE GOLDEN GATE

Foreword and Keynote Sermon by
BILLY GRAHAM

CRUSADE AT THE GOLDEN GATE

Sherwood Eliot Wirt

HARPER & BROTHERS NEW YORK

CRUSADE AT THE GOLDEN GATE

Wirt, Sherwood Eliot.
    Crusade at the Golden Gate.   Foreword and keynote
sermon by Billy Graham.   ₁1st ed.₎   New York, Harper
₍1959₎

    176 p.   21 cm.

    A report on Billy Graham's evangelistic campaign in San Francisco,
April 27–June 22, 1958.

    1. Graham, William Franklin, 1918-   2. Revivals—San Fran-
cisco.   I. Title.

BV3785.G69W5   269.20979461   59–7163 ‡

Library of Congress

FOR THE PRAISING OF HIS NAME

CONTENTS

7

CONTENTS

8

FOREWORD

In the main this report on the San Francisco Crusade deals with that which is of greatest importance in any evangelistic campaign: the spiritual impact upon human lives.

I have always contended that the capacity crowds, the array of statistics, and the smoothness of organization are of little import unless men and women have an effective and lasting encounter with Jesus Christ.

Sherwood Wirt has captured the heartbeat of the Crusades by bringing to the witness stand those who can say, "We believe, not because of thy saying: for we have heard

Him ourselves, and know that this is indeed the Christ, the Savior of the world."

In a world that has become discouraged at its own efforts to redeem itself, it is good to know that "there hath not failed one word of all His good promise," and that no one ever came to God in sincerity who was disappointed.

May this book, along with our faltering labors of love, be for the honor and Glory of Jesus Christ, our Lord and Savior.

BILLY GRAHAM

PREFACE

The preparing of these pages has been an inspiring and rewarding experience. To see the full scope of a Billy Graham Crusade in action is to realize its uniqueness in the spiritual life of our time. To watch Dr. Graham and his team and staff at work, and to talk with those whose lives have been touched by the Crusade's message, is a privilege for which I shall ever be grateful to God.

Only God knows the full story of what happened in the San Francisco Bay Area during the momentous days between April 27 and June 22, 1958. What has been caught in this report is a mere fragment. It would be better perhaps not to speak of a report at all, for while I have sought to be objective, it is hard for a minister to be dispassionate when God is obviously and tremendously at work. More appropriately this book could be called an American testimony of praise and thanksgiving, or a few bars from the Hallelujah Chorus, sung robustly and with the barest suggestion of western rhythm.

The story of such a Crusade must reflect the opinions of many people, and it would be hard to name all those whose enthusiasms, sympathy, and critical interest have helped to shape the chapters. I must, however, thank a few persons for their special help. Dr. Graham's gracious introduction and his warm support from the beginning of the undertaking are gladly acknowledged. Among his associates I wish particularly to thank for their kind offices Dr. Walter H. Smyth, Walter F. Bennett, Fred Dienert, Miss Sarah Jepson, Miss Patricia Campion, Dr. Charles Farah, Charles Riggs, Russ Reed, Miss Muriel Bergstrom, and other members of the San Francisco staff. Fellow pastors who gave valued advice included Dr. Robert B. Munger, Dr. Carl G. Howie, Rev. Donald F. Lehmann, Rev. Ernest L. Hastings, Rev. Ross F. Hidy, Rev. Hugh David Burcham, Rev. Robert Murphy, and Rev. John Lucas. To brother pastors who lent encouragement and prayer support I shall always be grateful. I am indebted to the libraries of the Oakland *Tribune*, the San Francisco *Chronicle*, and the San Francisco *Call-Bulletin*, among others, and particularly to the Rev. Bill Rose, church editor of the *Tribune*, for helpful assistance.

For permission to use special material I am obligated to the above-mentioned newspapers and to the magazine *Christianity Today*, for which I served as Crusade correspondent; to Dr. Graham, to the Rev. Leighton Ford, and to those whose stories appear (altered to avoid identification) in Chapter 4. For additional assistance I wish to thank Mrs. Harold Gudnason, Mrs. Lewis H. Monk, Mrs. C. Henry Johnson, Miss Carolyn Loos, Miss Helen McCain, Mrs. David M. Jolliffe, and Clifford A. Amaral. The use of the Plemmons family cottage at Paradise Park for the task of writing proved a real blessing.

My deep appreciation goes to my wife, Helen Winola, whose loving help is evident on every page and whose prayers kept me going; and to our son, Alexander, who cheerfully gave up a summer's vacation to the task. Finally I would acknowledge the indulgence of the good people of Hillside Presbyterian Church, many of whom were with me at the Cow Palace night after night. What the Crusade did for our East Oakland parish in a few short months is a story by itself. I am only one of many pastors in the Bay Area today whose vision seems clearer and whose task feels lighter.

S.E.W.

The Manse
Oakland, California
January, 1959

CHAPTER I · THE PLACE

San Francisco, the lovely, carefree Girl of the Golden West
—who can describe her? "One of the world's most unusual
cities," attempts Herb Caen, "gleaming like a jewel on the
western shore of America . . . a compact, teeming metropolis of 800,000 people compressed into 44 square miles at
the tip of a peninsula, surrounded on two sides by the greatest landlocked harbor in the world and on the third by the
boundless Pacific."[1]

Unusual? Yes, because it is a city of paradoxes with a
"schizoid personality." Not only is there the matter of the

[1] *New Guide to San Francisco*, New York, Doubleday, 1957.

weather—warm and cool, sunny and foggy at the same time. It is also "at once incredibly ugly and incredibly beautiful, as American as Mark Twain yet as international as Hong Kong; as western as its redwoods yet the greatest melting pot in America."[2] The better one knows it, the more its contradictions multiply. "It is an unreasonable city. . . . It loves the good as well as the evil. It is unfaithful to both. It makes enemies of everybody and it loves everybody."[3]

Today the clanging, Disneylandish cable cars battle for the right-of-way with sleek Cadillacs prowling up Powell Street. Tarnished gingerbread houses look ghostly and venerable alongside the audacious new architecture. San Francisco is not an old city, but so tempestuous and so romantic have been her hundred years of history that every block seems to be steeped in lore, while an old-world flavor clings inescapably to the whole. It has been said that there are really only two cities in the United States: New York and San Francisco. Will Irwin called it "the gayest, most light-hearted city in the western hemisphere." William Howard Taft called it "the city that knows how."

The people of San Francisco are easily distinguished along the western slope. To the traditional hospitality and friendliness of the coast they add a touch of urbanity, of unconventional conventionality, of tasteful dress and sophisticated air. It may be the gloves they wear, or the hour they retire. It may be their trace of "south-of-the-slot" accent. In one way or another San Franciscans manage to differ from the southern Californians, from the Valley people, even from the folks across the Bay—and have done so for a century. In their own way they seem to resemble more the Londoners and the Parisians. "What is supremely important to San

[2] A. Valentine, *Vigilante Justice*, New York, Reynal, 1956.
[3] William Saroyan, intro. to *San Francisco*, New York, Longmans, 1939.

16

Franciscans is that they be let alone to think and act as they please."[4] They are also a proud people, proud of their bridges and their breath-taking vistas, proud of their salty and flamboyant past, proud that their city gave birth to the United Nations.

It has been said that San Francisco will be whatever a person himself wishes it to be. Within its small compass are housed many diverse cultures, the Chinese world of China-town, the Italian world of the North Beach, the Russian world of Potrero Hill, the Negro world around Sutter and Fillmore, plus a healthy dispersion of Irish, Japanese, German, Scandinavian, Mexican, French and other peoples. Says William Saroyan, "San Francisco is the whole world recreated as a single work of art: a painting, a work of sculpture, a poem, a symphony, a story. It is the whole world brought together for the eye of man to behold and the heart to understand."[5]

What has made San Francisco so charming in some eyes, however, has been a matter of continued concern and dismay in other eyes, including the eyes of Christians. The sins of the world, the flesh and the devil have afflicted the City by the Golden Gate from its birth far more violently than any other metropolis of modern history. Twice the corruption in government and general disrespect for law and order forced the decent citizenry to by-pass their elected officials and to form Vigilance Committees for the protection of the city and the re-establishment of justice.

Not only did the city grow too fast—from 50 or 60 inhabitants in the summer of 1846 to 50,000 some five years later—it grew with the wrong kind of constituents: un-

[4] *San Francisco* (Federal Writers' Project), New York, Hastings House, 1947, p. 94.
[5] *Op. cit.*

scrupulous politicians from New York's Tammany district, convicts from Australia, gamblers from all over the world who flocked to San Francisco to feast off the pay of the Forty-Niners. Murder and dueling in the city streets became common; the indifference of authorities to the flourishing vice and narcotics trade made San Francisco known to some at least as "the wickedest city in the world."

Against the unhealthy forces at work down the years there has been a group of earnest, devoted citizens who have banded together in a sustained effort to give their city good government. Carrying on where the Vigilantes left off, yet without stepping outside the existing legal processes, these men and women time after time have pushed through reforms in civic administration, and have forced the cleaning up of disorderly spots. Further, they have given to the city an international reputation as a place of culture and beauty. They have improved its schools, its libraries and its parks. They rebuilt the city after earthquake and fire, attracted industry and commerce, and staged two world's fairs. To them goes the palm for having made of San Francisco a city that people would rather visit than any other in the world.

Yet something is missing. Nearly every other sizable city in America has been born out of a strong Christian witness which has helped to shape the city's character. One thinks of John Cotton in early Boston, William Penn in Philadelphia, Peter Frelinghuysen in New York, Lord Baltimore in Baltimore, Dwight L. Moody in Chicago—to name only a few. No matter how perverse the elements that later crept in, our American cities by and large have never been able completely to shake off their heritage. A godly principle still exercises a conservative restraint over the atmosphere of the municipality.

But San Francisco has never known that kind of ordered Christian conscience. The city's earliest beginnings are steeped in sacred tradition as the Mission Dolores was founded by Father Junipero Serra and the Franciscans in 1776. However, by the time the miners arrived the Mexican government had long since confiscated the mission lands and the buildings had fallen into neglect. Far from exerting influence for good on the mushrooming city, the mission had become a popular scene of Sunday bear and bull fights. Roman Catholics who came west with the gold rush had to build their work from scratch like the rest, until in 1857 the mission buildings were restored to the Church. Thus St. Francis gave his name, but never his spirit, to the brawling young city. Likewise the Mormons who sailed around the Horn and settled in Yerba Buena (later San Francisco) in 1846 were overwhelmed and scattered within three years by the influx of gold-seekers, and their leader, Sam Brannan, defected from the rule of Brigham Young. By 1850 the Presbyterians, Methodists, Baptists, Congregationalists, Unitarians and Jews had all established footholds in the city, but they were tiny pockets difficult to find in the general hubbub, and even more difficult to be heard.

What, in the absence of a strong Christian environment, did serve to shape the city? Already we have spoken of the deep desire of many people to work for and to establish social order. For the rest of the easygoing citizenry there are Josiah Royce's contemptuous words—"irresponsibility, insufferable laziness, detestable good nature and carelessly criminal tolerance." Most of those who came west were more interested in building quick fortunes than in rearing enduring cities. Even good men winked at shocking conditions, and many a Christian shook his head when he should have raised his voice. If a member of the "Hounds" (who tormented the nonwhite populace in 1849) was elected sheriff, what was anyone expected to do about it? If a man made his living contracting to cut off people's noses, how could you stop a thing like that?

There were three voices that were raised for righteousness in early San Francisco, loudly enough to be heard above the noise of the gaming tables. One belonged to "Father" William Taylor, the stronghearted Methodist street-preacher of the early 'fifties whose fearless proclamation of the Gospel always commanded a hearing, and whose passion to win men to Jesus Christ stands like a rock in a weary land. Another was James King "of William," the crusading founder-editor of the *Bulletin*, who thundered for justice in his columns, and who exposed criminal elements in government so mercilessly that he was shot by one of the city's supervisors, thereby bringing about the formation of the second Vigilance Committee. The third was the Rev. Thomas Starr King, the Unitarian minister whose silver tongue and flaming spirit led in securing the state's loyalty to the Union during the Civil War years.

Eliminate these voices from the city's history, and how curiously mute the Church seems to have been! Not that the local congregations have been inactive; on the contrary, from earliest times they have preached the Word, administered the sacraments and have done an effective work as they were given light and were able. San Francisco's pastors have been well described as "faithful, intelligent, laborious and devout." It is not criticism but historical statement to say that the churches have not significantly affected the City by the Golden Gate. The Vigilance Committee of 1856, for example, was Church-endorsed but not Church-led. It drew its motivation not from the sword of the Spirit and the prophetic message of Scripture, but simply from a situation which decent men had found to be intolerable. The Church has not been ranged on the side of the Gospel against its environment; too often it has been quietly absorbed by its environment. Thus one honest present-day minister of a large city church has suggested that what the pastors have done for San Francisco may not be as significant as what San Francisco has done to the pastors.

In 1856 W. P. Strickland observed, "Numerous as have been the works published in relation to California, its religious history has not been written." Another hundred years have passed and that history still has not been written —a significant fact in itself. Meanwhile the spate of books published about California has grown to a figure hard to estimate. Who has written those books? Not the Church! The typical book about San Francisco could not be ascribed to a Christian hand by any stretch of the imagination. Almost without exception the chroniclers have skirted the moral issues; they have smirked at the city's "colorful" past, and shed nostalgic tears over the passing of such "landmarks" as the Barbary Coast, and have concluded their studies by setting forth what they consider to be the principles of proper conduct for a San Franciscan: equability; holding one's liquor well; tolerance; not slapping people on the back; good taste and form; and get the job done. "This do," they tell us, "and thou shalt live."

It is disturbing to learn that the whole task of interpreting the spirit and purpose of San Francisco has been taken over by "intellectuals" who are at heart romanticists, hedonists and epicures, while the God-fearing men and women burrow ever more deeply in the life of their particular church programs as if to say, "The situation is out of control." The present irruption of the "Beat Generation" illustrates the point. San Francisco has long had its art and literary colony, fairly unrelated to the things of Christ. Today many tourists "doing the city" will not so much as cast a glance at an historic church, but they would not miss seeing "The Place" where the "beatniks" gather for anything.

What is a "beatnik"? Being beat, we are told,

> is leaning on the dusty bar of a bistro and saying softly, 'I don't believe in God or in Billy Graham either. Today's messiahs are all in the loony bins. . . .' It is getting high at marijuana parties or deliriously intoxicated with a sharpened awareness of sights and sounds and smells.[6]

What is the philosophy of a "beatnik"? It is, "I'm here and I wish I weren't and to hell with it." Or, if a "loner" who is "aware" is asked what life is all about, we are told that he will reply, "I don't know, I don't care, and it doesn't make any difference."

Yet to all this the Church says nothing—is hardly aware the problem exists. If "Father" Taylor were alive today he would not be preaching from the pulpit of the wealthy downtown church; he would be in front of "The Place" singing up a meeting, and confronting the nihilism of the "beat" ones with a gospel of redemption and hope through the Lord Jesus Christ. There is in fact a curious modernity about Taylor's lament over the spiritual state of the primitive city in his classic, *Seven Years' Street Preaching in San Francisco*:[7]

> This city, it is true, can exhibit as many church edifices at a greater cost than any other city of its age in the world. The people of California are justly proverbial for their liberality in giving for charitable and religious purposes. They also treat a man's religious opinions, professions and efforts with more respect, probably, than any other new country; and a minister of the Gospel can preach in the open streets of any city or town in California, day or night,

[6] Allen Brown in the San Francisco *Chronicle*, June 15, 1958.
[7] New York, Carlton & Porter, 1856, 342.

without any fear of serious disturbance. Everybody, to be sure, will not stop and listen, but nobody will stop to interfere with him. But, with all these admissions in favor of California in general, and of San Francisco in particular, I believe nevertheless that it is as yet the hardest country in this world in which to get sinners converted to God.

More recently William Saroyan has unconsciously disclosed how San Francisco "patronizes" its churches and their message. In his advice to tourists he recommends:

> There are no end of ways of enduring time [!] in San Francisco, pleasantly, beautifully, and with the romance of living in everything. Eat any kind of dish the races of the world know how to prepare. Drink any kind of wine you like. Play any game you care to play. Go to the opera. The symphony. The concert. Go to a movie or a stage play. Loaf around in the high-toned bars, or in the honky-tonks. Sail in the bay. Go down to Bay Meadows or Tanforan and bet the horses. *Go to church.*[8]

But lest anyone think that San Francisco is a city of churches, George West hastens to reassure that "nowhere in America is there less in evidence the cold theological eye [!], the cautious hand withheld, the lifted eyebrow, the distrust of playfulness. . . ."[9]

What are the reasons for the difficulty of the field from a Christian point of view? Taylor in his early work mentions some of them: the isolated condition of society, the migratory character of the population, and the basic attraction of material gain. Just one hundred and one years later, in December, 1957, a study of the problem was made by the Rev. Leighton Ford, associate evangelist with the Billy Graham team, in preparation for the 1958 San Francisco

[8] *Op. cit.,* vii. *(Italics added.)*
[9] *San Francisco, op. cit.,* 93.

Bay Cities Crusade. Mr. Ford's survey, while wider in scope, bears an interesting resemblance to the remarks of the pioneer street-preacher. Because of its relevance to the purposes of this book, I am quoting from Mr. Ford's study at some length:

> What are some of the major problems faced by church groups in the Bay Area?
>
> 1. *Mobility*. In the next twelve months there will be one change of address for every two families. A telephone executive estimates that only one out of three phones will be connected to the same address for a full year. There is a tremendous desire to move, an unsettled feeling. The pastor faces people who give this excuse: "No, I won't find a church home now, because I expect to move in several months," even though eventually they may never move.
>
> 2. *Money*. New churches are needed to reach the 8,200 new people coming in every month. The land alone for a new church costs $40,000. People who have moving in the back of their minds won't invest in land for a church they soon expect to leave.
>
> 3. *Lapsed Members*. There is a saying among church leaders, "That's not snow on the Sierras. Those are church letters people threw out the window as they drove into California." One official estimates that 60 to 80 per cent of people coming to California are church members back home, but that only 15 per cent join here. It indicates perhaps that to many of them church membership was a traditional part of the pattern of their community life, and did not involve a personal commitment to Christ.
>
> 4. *Pagan Background*. The pagan spirit of '49 still dominates. Much of the rest of the country was settled by people looking for a way of life which included family and church. But California was settled by people who were seeking for only one thing—money. Stores and mines,

but not churches, were at the center of the towns. *San Francisco has never had a great influential church*. The city has no religious heritage of any significance.

5. *No Community*. There is no community spirit out here as in the Midwest. It is pioneer and independent in spirit. People from other parts of the country came from towns where there was a community tradition, including church, but all the ties have been broken as they are uprooted to the West Coast. San Francisco has always been a city, but not a community; with masses, but not individuals. There has been little neighborly spirit—the neighborly spirit of the other communities is bought and sold here. There is an indifference to need such as in New York, where a person can fall into the gutter or on the street and no one stops to help—and no one cares about the indifference. Here is a splendid open door for the Church to provide a community that cares.

6. *Ignorance of Christ*. There are many people, non-whites and foreign-born whites, in the San Francisco area who are ignorant of the Christian message. There are also many American-born people who have been here a long time and as a result have never had the slightest Christian training. These people are either indifferent or hostile to the Church. They are lost and bewildered, they try to escape their problems by dope or drink or money or pleasure, but it never occurs to them that Christ might have the answer.

One is inevitably reminded in considering San Francisco of Laodicea. That was a great city which stood at the crossroads of communication and transportation. It thought itself to be rich and in need of nothing. But Jesus said that Laodicea, although it was a banking center was poor, although it was noted for its manufacture of cloth was naked, and although it was the home of the famous medical school, was blind.[10] He counseled the city to get from

[10] Rev. 3:17-18.

God gold tried in the fire, a robe of righteousness, and spiritual eye-salve. The great sin of Laodicea like that of San Francisco was indifference. They couldn't care less. The same Jesus Christ says to San Francisco today as He did to Laodicea then, "Behold, I stand at the door, and knock. . . ."[11] Jesus Christ has been left standing too long on Mount Davidson. He wants to be received into the heart of the people and of the city.

The present-day statistics of San Francisco's social habits accentuate the nature of the problem. At the time of the Billy Graham Crusade the San Francisco *Call-Bulletin* published current figures indicating that the national average of alcoholics in 1957 was 4,390 per 100,000 population. By contrast, the state of California's alcoholism rate was 7,060 per 100,000, and the city of San Francisco posted a shocking 16,760, or nearly four times the national average.

Suicides in San Francisco totaled 195 in 1957, about two and one-half times the national suicide rate of 9.7 per 100,000 population. In the fiscal year ending in June, 1957, San Francisco reported 76,202 marriage licenses issued, and 42,834 divorce complaints filed, of which 29,578 resulted in final divorce decrees. As for churchgoing, San Francisco's church membership is presently reported at about 17 per cent compared with the national average of about 60 per cent, while her church attendance on a given Sunday is reported as low as 7 per cent of the population.

Into San Francisco each day there come some two hundred thousand persons who will sleep elsewhere that night. Some are tourists on the move, but a large proportion of them are commuters who have preferred to make their homes outside of the city proper. The moment one travels

[11] Rev. 3:20.

out of the metropolitan area into the suburbs, or over the bridges to the cities across the Bay, he finds himself in a different world. Vanished are the dazzle, the cosmopolitan air and the old-world charm. Gone too are the unenviable statistics of the big city—first in liquor consumption, in alcoholism, in suicides, in cigarette consumption, in single-person dwellings, in sex crimes. Instead one finds swarms of children, baby-sitters, trees, sunshine, super-markets, bridge parties, churches, conventional habits and western neighborliness.

The entrepreneurs of 1849 did not deem it advisable to set up saloons and music halls in the bucolic fields that are now San Rafael, Piedmont and Burlingame, so that these communities were given time to develop normally, along with scores of other Bay Area towns. Today the streets of Richmond, El Cerrito, Orinda, Alameda, Albany, Redwood City, Palo Alto, Sunnyvale, San Carlos, Hayward, San Mateo, Walnut Creek, Concord, Petaluma, San Anselmo, Fairfax and other localities are dotted with flourishing churches. In the West, however, mushrooming membership is not necessarily an index to spiritual health. The spiritual problems of the greater San Francisco Bay region are substantially the spiritual problems of American suburbia. Those problems differ from San Francisco's but are none the less real.

Sociologists have shown us that Suburban Man is tempted to pick up his religion, like his golf swing, from his peers. They have also suggested that the First Church of Rolling Knolls may offer a plethora of "togetherness" and "belongingness," but be in short supply on the Gospel that is the power of God unto salvation. In the city of Berkeley, across the Bay from "The City," there are no less than seven accredited theological training schools, while elsewhere around the Bay are numerous Bible schools and colleges. Enrollments are up and scholarship is keen, but some schools are not speaking to one another, and there is wide disagreement over the Bible. The very words "saved" and "lost" threaten to become antiquarian. The proliferation of sects in the midst suggests that something is amiss in the church life. Of those who made decisions at the San Francisco Billy Graham Crusade, a majority were from towns around the fringe of the Bay—which suggests that whatever the meaning of the present boom in "religiosity," it has not yet kindled a holy fire in the churches.

Now that the picture has been drawn and the problem set forth, we need to ask soberly whether any mass evangelistic effort could be envisioned as leading toward a solution. Could an "invasion" by Billy Graham and his team—or anyone else—be expected to bring about desirable character changes in the community? If San Francisco, Oakland, and the other cities have not listened to their own faithful shepherds over the years, why should they be expected to listen to an outsider?

Historically "revival meetings" have never made an impression on the Bay Area. Taylor's strenuous efforts brought meager results. Dwight L. Moody made a brief trip west, but so did many others, and the sands have covered their tracks. Charles Templeton attempted to awaken the city of Oakland in more recent times, under impressive sponsorship, but he left discouraged. The inability of the churches of the area to unite around any single effort has been a persistent stumbling block and has helped to make the Bay region known as "the graveyard of evangelism."

There is no tradition in the area that would lead the people to expect anything of mass evangelism. Contrary to the East Coast, the South and the Midwest, spiritual awakening has never come to the Pacific Coast in any full-bodied way.

For native Californians, therefore, revival was something they had heard about, just as they had heard about Billy Graham. They did not necessarily oppose an evangelistic "crusade" any more than they opposed a visit from Mars. They just had never had one. Even dedicated Christian people were questioning whether they should rearrange their schedules for May and June of 1958. Leaving aside such usual counterattractions as television, gardening, building projects, social engagements, and family life, how could one be expected to shelve his regular church obligations for several weeks of protracted meetings at a point several miles away?

Yet there were also some things that could be said positively. Ever since a chance luncheon meeting between Dr. Abbott Book, executive secretary of the Northern California-Nevada Council of Churches, and Dr. Robert Boyd Munger, pastor of the First Presbyterian Church of Berkeley and newly-returned from the 1954 London Crusade, there had been devoted and dedicated men working to bring Billy Graham to San Francisco. The executive committee of pastors and laymen found upon inquiry that over three hundred churches of the area were eager to support such a Crusade. A burden of prayer was given to the churches, and spontaneous prayers continued for over two years. The press and the public seemed interested. Dr. Graham's brief visit in November, 1954, when he spoke to 14,000 in San Francisco's Civic Auditorium, revealed a hunger on the part of many for a closer walk with God.

Such in all too brief compass is the background of the meetings that commenced in San Francisco's Cow Palace in the spring of the Year of Grace 1958. It now becomes our task to examine briefly the man who led those meetings, William Franklin Graham; together with his message, his organization, and his Crusade.

CHAPTER II ▪ THE MAN

The man Billy Graham is already one of the best-known figures of the mid-century period, and has become the subject of innumerable books and articles. This chapter does not seek to revise or repeat what has been written heretofore, but will present Graham only as he was seen in the San Francisco area in 1958. In the light of the preceding pages, it can be understood that the Bay region faced the evangelist with a challenge of classic proportions. St. George against the dragon had nothing on Dr. Graham against the spiritual torpor of San Francisco. Nevertheless I do not wish to imply that there was no contest. Billy Graham's gifts of the Spirit are considerable, and he is no mean antagonist for the Lord. He understood something of the nature of his opponent: even before he reached California Graham was making comments on San Francisco's suicide, alcoholism and divorce statistics that had newsmen scurrying to the libraries.[1]

"God loves this rebel city, loves foemen brisk and game," wrote a poet of San Francisco's past,[2] but except for some bad moments in the spring of 1906, the "foemen" have pretty much had it their own way. Reform mayors and honest police chiefs have always had to buck the insouciance and whimsy of the public, which seems almost to take pride in its sins. So it was that when 1958 brought major league baseball to the City by the Golden Gate, it also brought the first championship match on the moral issue in over one hundred years. Our task is to examine what happened when Billy Graham came west to proclaim repentance and salvation to a people who, by and large, were looking for something else.

Billy was not really rested when he arrived in San Francisco. Only a few weeks before he had concluded a strenuous tour through the West Indies and Central America, and neither he nor his colleagues were in top physical condition. A few days' golfing at Palm Springs helped, but the interruptions were many and the burdened souls were hard to avoid even on the fairways. Now he faced a minimum of six weeks' uninterrupted preaching in the Cow Palace, a back-breaking social calendar and outside-speaking schedule, a low level of spiritual interest, separation from his wife and five children, daily problems of harmonious

[1] See p. 26.
[2] Vachel Lindsay, *The City That Would Not Repent*, in *General William Booth and Other Poems*, New York, Harper, 1916.

relationships with team, executive committee, staff, press, public, pastors and churches, radio and television, and various business firms; daily newspaper columns to write and questions to answer; weekly international broadcasts to prepare, and Saturday night telecasts to 175 stations coast-to-coast in the United States and Canada: "the largest audience in the history of the Christian Church."

The San Francisco Crusade, from the view of the team and the executive committee of local ministers and laymen, developed much as did its predecessors. The more familiar techniques that were so well described in the books that followed the London, Glasgow and New York Crusades were also used in San Francisco. There is no real need to repeat them here. Night after night the team, counselors, ushers and choir members were on duty at the Cow Palace. Morning after morning the prayer partners were meeting in homes to ask for divine power and guidance for the Crusade. Day after day the executive committee continued its behind-the-scenes task of rallying support, raising money and making decisions. The geographical setting was different and the people were different, but the procedure was the same.

To discover what happened in San Francisco it is best to go to the beginning. On Saturday morning, April 26, 1958, Billy Graham arrived by train from Los Angeles and was driven to the Hotel Californian, where he held a press conference.

At the conference he carefully parried questions that might be blown up into headlines. Was San Francisco such a sinful city? Well, there were statistics; but he was not prepared to say it was more sinful than other cities. Did he know the attitude of the Roman Catholics? The Roman

Carl Bigelow, Oakland Tribune

Billy Graham arrives at railroad depot for start of San Francisco Crusade, April 27, 1958, and is met by Crusade Director Walter Smyth (left), Co-Chairman Carl Howie (wearing hat) and Prayer Chairman George Bostrom (right), among others.

At press conference in Californian Hotel, Graham explains his motives and his hopes in coming to San Francisco.

Roy Williams, Oakland Tribune

Popular features of the Crusade were ministers' "breakfast workshops," at which team members spoke. Graham chats with pastors at Sheraton Palace Hotel.

Key figures in the Crusade: (left t right) Co-Chairmen W. Earle Smith an Carl Howie; soloist George Beverly She Lorin Whitney, organist; (seated) Ted Smith, pianist, with Crusade choir song book.

Five of the team's six associate evangelists: (left to right) Grady Wilson, Leighton Ford, Howard Jones, Ralph Mitchell and Akbar Abdul Haqq.

Best-known of Billy Graham's associates is his master of ceremonies and choir director, Cliff Barrows, rehearsing here with choir of nearly 2000 voices in Cow Palace.

Howard Erker, Oakland Tribune

Martin J. Cooney, Oakland Tribune

Part of the soprano section of the vast choir that sang nightly throughout the Crusade.

The congregation in the Cow Palace joined with the choir in the singing of familiar hymns.

Russ Reed, Oakland Tribune

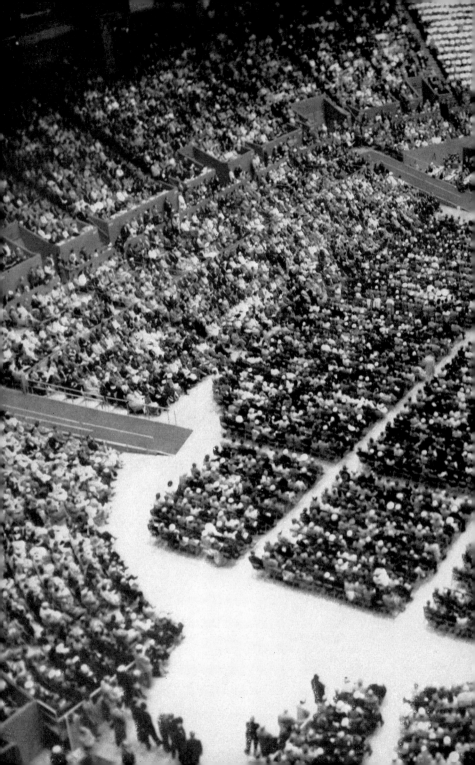

Scene at the opening of the Crusade in the Cow Palace on Sunday afternoon, April 27, 1958. Five thousand were turned away. Inside were eighteen thousand.

Russ Reed, Oakland Tribune

The Bible is never far from Graham's words or hands as he preaches.

Graham steps outside Cow Palace to address the overflow crowd.

Delegation of Luther Lea-
guers listens to Graham at
Cow Palace.

Graham points to cut flowers
to illustrate a spiritual truth,
in sermon at Cow Palace.

Old as well as young hear the
message of the Gospel.

Church had never officially opposed his Crusades. How long would he be there? He did not know; at least until June 8. That afternoon Dr. Graham was established in the Villa Motor Hotel in San Mateo, and on the following day he opened his Crusade.

The Cow Palace is located a few hundred yards south of the city boundary, in an indentation in the hills known as Visitacion Valley. It has a colorful history—during one season 150,000 paid to watch Sonja Henie and her ice skaters —but never had the huge auditorium been impressed into such use as this. Now all things were ready; ushers had been briefed, counselors trained and dedicated, the great choir rehearsed. Cliff Barrows, chorister extraordinary and master of ceremonies, stepped to the microphone at exactly three o'clock on Sunday afternoon, April 27, 1958, and remarked in his genial and familiar way, "Good afternoon, ladies and gentlemen, welcome to the Cow Palace and the San Francisco Bay Cities Crusade . . ."

The town was a bit shaken by that first Sunday. Even with Willie Mays and the Giants offering a counterattraction in Seals Stadium, the Cow Palace was jammed with 18,000 sitting and standing. Five thousand more were turned away, and Billy had to go outside to address them. The police, used to surly catcalls from disappointed sports fans, were pleasantly surprised when the overflow crowd refused to complain. After Graham's brief address to them, an invitation was given; hands were raised, and counselors went to work.

Graham then returned inside to find that the meeting was under way. The western folk were responding to the pleasant manners of Song Leader Barrows as had the people of London and Madras. They had prayed, they had listened to the music of George Beverly Shea, Tedd Smith and Lorin

Whitney, and had heard words of greeting from local dignitaries. Yet there was no doubt as to whom the people had come to hear. The mantle of greatness hung upon one man, and for him they waited—whether for curiosity, or hero worship, or hunger for truth.

They were not disappointed. A six-foot, two-and-a-half-inch, broad-shouldered figure stepped to the pulpit and announced, "I'm going to ask that there be no walking around, no moving of any kind, no talking. One person moving in a great auditorium like this can distract many people. There are some here today who have burdens that need to be lifted, problems that need to be solved, sins that need to be forgiven. While I am talking to you, another voice down inside of you will be speaking. That voice will be the Spirit of God. Tell me, when has the Bay Area ever had a moment like this? They are praying for you in Afghanistan . . ."

The people seemed to settle back with a sigh as there ensued one of the more remarkable preaching demonstrations in the history of the Church: a simple setting forth of the critical need of the modern world, and the power of the Gospel to meet that need. Those who listened to Whitefield, Spurgeon and Moody have said that their written sermons do not convey the power of the message as they spoke it. The sermon Graham preached that afternoon is included in this volume exactly as it was delivered, but it does not re-create the event. On the platform behind the man as he spoke were Christian leaders of ability and attainment: the Rev. Carl G. Howie, Ph.D., author and archaeologist; Dr. Akbar Abdul Haqq, educator, theologian and evangelist whose zeal for Christ had aroused opposition in India; the Rev. Joseph Blinco of London, skillful phrase-master, one of the great voices of British Methodism; Dr. Sandford

Fleming, president emeritus of Berkeley Baptist Divinitiy School, and Dr. Harold Graves, president of Golden Gate Baptist Theological Seminary; Dean C. Julian Bartlett of Grace Cathedral; and with them two dozen theologically trained ministers—doctors of divinity, of theology, of philosophy—listening to this evangelist who had never attended a seminary.

What they heard was not as profound as many of the books on their shelves at home. Each message Billy preached was substantially the same. It was said of Archbishop Temple that one never knew where His Grace would begin, but was always sure where he would end; and it was so with Billy Graham. There might be a well-told joke, or a Bible story, painted on a wide canvas with bright colors, or a string of Scriptural quotations, deliberately read from his notes. There was an exposition of the Word and an analysis of the present situation; and always the closing invitation. Some pastors, remembering their own efforts of the morning, might have felt a little let down.

But not the people! They had found at last (so they seemed to suggest) a man to whom they could listen, who knew what life was all about; one who spoke their language and who did not mince words. If he failed to use an ostentatious vocabulary, he achieved clarity. If he missed the profundity of the pundit, he made it up in liberty of delivery. He did not stand in the pulpit like a stick. He was a man, flinging out his long arms, pacing the platform, crouching, peering, then standing erect with finger uplifted. His Bible was his touchstone; he picked it up and laid it down twenty times. When he clinched a point, it seemed to be hammered home with the nails of God; and even while he was making it, his mind was racing on to the next phrase, the next sentence, the next point. He needed no breather to push his thought ahead, no homiletic punctuation such as, "My friends," "dearly beloved," "Brethren," "Oh, yes," "Oh, listen," "On the other hand," or the pious pause and the discreet glance downward to the notes. His ideas were carried close to the memory-surface and were called up easily. His sense of the incongruous was so keen that he seemed able to lift a comical story from nowhere to liven the body of the message.

The message was always about sin. Not the sin of the Russians, but the sin of the Americans. Not the sins of those who were sitting in the theater or the ball park, but the sins of those who were in the Cow Palace. There was something fascinatingly shocking about the way Billy Graham "told them off"; their pastors had not dared talk to them like this. It was like going back to mother's knee, or father's!—and hearing again a parental lecture: "Some things are right to do, and some things are wrong, and you have been doing wrong. You thought you could get away with it but you can't. You've been caught, and there's only one thing to do, and that is to admit it. You may have had your own people fooled; you may have had your minister fooled; but now you've been found out. God has tracked you down. You're guilty." That's what he seemed to be saying.

There was tremendous audacity to the message, tremendous authority, and yet it was accepted meekly because of the nature of the person who spoke. The people seemed aware that this was no ordinary person, but a modern prophet sent from God. They knew he was modest—so much so that his organization suffered for it. They knew he was not seeking control over their lives or their money; that he practiced what he preached better than most; that his message was only the message of Scripture. They knew that he was no hot-eyed fanatic, but a relaxed Southern gentleman with good manners and more poise than most psychiatrists. They knew that he was no phony, that he couldn't help it if he had blond hair—what should he do? Wear a tonsure?

"You people have been so gracious in receiving us," said Billy, and they loved him by the thousands, and they loved his hair and they loved the Gospel he preached even though it made worms of them and made them face up to themselves as they hadn't done in years. Perhaps he would speak of the devil: "The devil will go to any length to gain a man's soul. He will offer any price to get it; but he doesn't have to offer anything much to get you because you'll sell out for chicken feed. The first little temptation that comes your way, and he's got you." Or he would speak of God: "God loves you. He loves you, He loves you, He loves you. He loves you so much that He sent His Son to die for you. On the Cross Jesus takes one hand from you and one hand from God and joins them together. You'll never come to God with your sins. He won't let you near Him; He is holy—but Jesus can take away your sins tonight. That's why I'm going to ask you to come down here and give your heart to Christ."

As he finished speaking, the choir began to sing softly. Members of the team left the platform and quietly directed the counselors toward inquirers of their own age and sex. Hundreds of people streamed down the aisles from all over the Cow Palace: ladies in fur stoles, lovers, ragged little children . . . Mexicans, Negroes, American Indians, Orientals . . . teenagers . . . the troubled ones, the curious ones, the uncommitted ones, the almost-persuaded ones, the surprised ones, the chastened ones. With the counselors they moved with slow dignity to an adjoining exhibit room for instruction. A few late ones got up from their seats and joined them, and still others fidgeted, wishing they had the nerve to do it. The evangelist turned for a final word to the thousands still waiting to be dismissed. "Ladies and gentlemen," he said, "I believe that what you have just seen represents the great hope of the world today."

From night to night the messages varied, yet always at their heart was some basic Christian doctrine. Visitors to the Cow Palace heard about justification, about reconciliation, about adoption, about the new birth, about the Holy Spirit, about the Trinity, about the sacraments, about heaven, about hell, about Satan, about the Second Advent of Jesus Christ, about the last judgment, about the dual nature of Christ, about the authority of Scripture, about the blood atonement and the centrality of the Cross. Nor were the social implications of the Gospel neglected; no one left the Cow Palace informed that he could love God without loving his neighbor. The evangelist inveighed against racial intolerance, bigotry, slum housing, character assassination, the arms race, communism, a foreign policy based on "self-interest," alcohol, and exploitation in labor relations. "As a Southerner, I used to consider Negroes were not my equal," he said, "but since I have become a Christian, I love them as I love members of my own family."

When Billy Graham first came to San Francisco in 1951 to attend a church convention he wore a ten-gallon sombrero, a cream-colored sport jacket, loud figured tie and blue suede shoes. Seven years had made their changes, not only in dress but in delivery.

There are many evidences that in the Cow Palace he achieved a maturity of message beyond anything he had ever done. He had slowed down the slightest bit, and his statements about Jesus Christ were less extreme and more seasoned with the experiences of life. Billy had said in Madison Square Garden in the summer of 1957 that "Christ does not remove your problems; your problems may be even greater after you come to Christ, but you will have a capacity and power to face them." He said it with deeper emphasis in San Francisco. If the whole world were to become Christian, he told his audiences, there would still be problems. "Even in a Christian home there are tensions —but Christ creates an atmosphere in which solutions can be worked out."

There was evident also a more discerning analysis of the motives of some of his listeners. Not everyone who came had a "hunger for God." And he seemed to show a new understanding of the ministers with whom he was working. "Some of the things I say will make you cringe," he told pastors gathered at a breakfast "workshop" during the first week. "Just close your ears and eyes and wait for something you can agree with. I cannot devise a theology that will please all of you, for we come from different backgrounds." His own background is strictly Southern: Associate Reformed Presbyterian of North Carolina; and since 1941, Southern Baptist.

When viewed in historical perspective, Graham's theology is in the main stream of the Christian faith. Many will contest the statement, but it is admitted by some of his liberal critics, and the general approval he has received around the world from Church leaders and laymen is sufficient evidence. Graham's Gospel is substantially the Gospel of St. Paul, John Chrysostom, Augustine, Wyclif, Hus, Luther, Calvin, Hooker and the early Puritans, the Wesleys, Carey and the great missionaries. Emphases may have differed but the basic material is the same: the fact of human sin, the penalty of death, the atoning sacrifice of Jesus Christ on the Cross, the resurrection, the new life in Christ, the return of the Lord, the Spirit, the Scriptures, the sacraments

—these have formed the hard core of the Church's faith down the centuries, and they make the framework of Graham's sermons. Whether his messages are "life-centered" and "socially relevant" are questions on which there are many opinions, but on the matter of historic Christianity there is really no debate.

As an itinerant evangelist Graham follows a vocational pattern which goes back to the New Testament, but with his well-known twentieth century flourishes. He is more polished than Billy Sunday, and he avoids the vivid death-bed scenes that D. L. Moody employed. He keeps away from John Wesley's trend toward a church within a church, or *ecclesiola in ecclesia*. Of all the noted evangelists since the Reformation he is probably closest to George White-field, for he shares with the seventeenth century's "Great Awakener" a strong doctrinal emphasis on the new birth, together with a zeal to reach the whole world and a gift of effective speech.

One secret of Billy Graham's power in San Francisco was his ability to bring Christians into touch with one another by omitting the things that divide them. There was a notable absence of the labels, clichés and stock phrases that Christians normally use to distinguish themselves. The word "Protestant," interestingly enough, was never once used in the Cow Palace.

An even more important secret was his appeal to youth. Probably the Holy Spirit's greatest work in the Crusade was done with young people. The seed of a new Christian commonwealth was planted on the West Coast as a result of the tremendous Thursday evening "Youth Nights," when the Cow Palace was always filled to capacity, and never less than a thousand came forward at the invitation.

Aisles were blocked clear to the rear of the auditorium. The eagerness with which the young people responded was strangely stirring. They loved Billy; they could "dig" him, and they seized enthusiastically upon the hope and purity that he held out to them in Jesus Christ.

Graham did not coddle the youth any more than he did the adults. When he spoke of sex he declared, "You'll never make it to the top until you lick this thing, and you'll never lick it without Christ." So they came: some from sophisticated church youth groups, amid the icy stares of their friends; some from juvenile halls where they had been given freedom to attend—duck-tailed young housebreakers and car stealers who could scarcely write their names, but who thumbed painfully through the Gospel of John for the first answer in "Lesson One: the Savior and Eternal Life." One boy came with his face ripped open after being thrown from a speeding hot-rod by his "friends." As they marched down the ramps the young westerners seemed to be telling the world that they would not be cozened out of their spiritual birthright by H-bombs or Hollywood or the devil himself.

What was it the man had? Advertisers called it "the hard sell," and one pharmaceutical firm ordered its salesmen to the Cow Palace to learn "how to put their message across." One of the young men learned his lesson so well that he registered a decision for Jesus Christ. Just before he came west Billy Graham learned that he had been voted America's "Salesman of the Year." San Francisco's noted columnist Herb Caen made a characteristic reference to Billy one morning in commenting on a report that the Giants were looking for a new pitcher: "Why don't they try Billy Graham? He's the best pitcher to appear in these parts in a long time."

There were others who called it not so much salesmanship as "mana," the mysterious stuff that clings to some unique individuals and makes them poets or witch doctors or geniuses or dictators or spellbinding evangelists, so we are told. "Mana" is a word derived from the peoples of Oceania and signifies a special kind of power. It is well known to psychologists and anthropologists, but because it is a fluid concept it is not easily explained. Californians had no difficulty in recognizing that there was something distinctive about the man. One spoke of the "organ tones" of his voice. Another decided that "listening to Billy Graham is like visiting the Grand Canyon for the first time." A thousand years ago he might have been a pillar saint to whom the world repaired for spiritual guidance; or one of the great ascetic missionaries, a Columba or a Boniface. The twentieth century has its own peculiar ways of recognizing a great man of God. Thus a waitress at the Ahwahnee Hotel in Yosemite Valley discreetly filled Billy's water glass and whispered, "I accepted the Lord at one of your meetings in Germany." And when he parked at a drive-in restaurant in Monterey, strangers left the counter and the adjacent cars to wander over with menus and paper napkins for him to "sign."

Some thought that Billy's real secret was his earnestness and sincerity. The evangelist did his best to disillusion them at that point, and told a well known football story to dispel the notion that God will honor any man as long as he is sincere. It was the story of Captain-elect Roy Riegels, the University of California center who picked up a fumble and sprinted confusedly toward his own goal line in the Rose Bowl game of January 1, 1930, against Georgia Tech. "He was the most earnest, sincere man you ever saw," Billy pointed out, "but he ran the wrong way and lost the game."

It is possible that one day a qualified person will attempt a serious psychograph of William Franklin Graham, a man who epitomizes many of the basic yearnings of our day. As a minister I would like to suggest that there are certain spiritual qualities in his makeup, which were evident at San Francisco, and which may go farther than any of the above interpretations in explaining the man's secret.

First, he has the anointing of the Holy Spirit, which is God's special preparation of a man who has been uniquely set apart to be His messenger.

Then he has prayer. Not only is his own life carefully nurtured in daily prayer; there are also millions praying for him. Forty prayer groups on the island of Trinidad alone were interceding on Billy's behalf for the San Francisco Crusade. Bob Pierce returned from Russia and reported at the Cow Palace that they were praying for San Francisco in Kiev and Moscow. Nearly every city in Australia had a Graham prayer group—for San Francisco. In India, in Germany, on Formosa it was the same story. Over 1,200 cottage prayer groups met Tuesday through Friday all around the shores of San Francisco Bay, listening to a Crusade devotional broadcast, then joining in asking God to bless the meetings; and they continued for two and one-half months.

He has a further quality best described as holiness. Few men in the twentieth century have possessed this gift, which can only come as the fruit of a thoroughly disciplined life, with much searching of the Scriptures and continuous communion with God. He told the graduating class of the Golden Gate Baptist Theological Seminary, "I read five of the Psalms each day as well as a chapter of Proverbs. These chapters teach me how to worship God and how to get along with my fellow men. I also read six pages from other books of the Bible daily in addition to my study in sermon preparation. If you will follow this procedure, you will read through Psalms and Proverbs every month and the Bible twice a year."

Another quality could be called perception in depth. It is a quality recognized by William Temple's biographer, Dr. Iremonger, in the archbishop, and he attributes it to a low threshold between the conscious and unconscious mind, so that thoughts of unusual wisdom and perceptivity came easily, even in casual conversation. Once on the platform at the Cow Palace, toward the end of the final week, I happened to be sitting next to Billy Graham and whispered to him, "Are you satisfied with the way the Crusade has been going?" The arena was jammed with people who had come to hear his message which would begin in a few moments, and I expected an answer such as, "Yes, on the whole," with a thoughtful nod of the head. Instead he said, "We are never satisfied, for we are always looking for deeper things." On another occasion in the brief press interview that took place each night before the meeting, a reporter asked Billy, "What would you say if I told you I was Jesus Christ?" The psychological implications of the question were tremendous, but Billy ignored them. "First," he said, "I would want to see the nail prints in your hands. Then since Jesus said He would come in glory, I'd like to see your glory."

Not so evident to the crowds, but clear to his intimates was the man's sacrificial nature. Billy Graham has paid a big price in separation from his family for long periods of time, and he paid it in San Francisco with tears of loneliness. Only the eldest daughter, thirteen-year-old Virginia, made the trip at the close of school. He has made a financial sacrifice, as is well known to his public. He has also made a sacrifice of health; ministers are often exhausted after preaching once or twice on Sunday, but Billy Graham in San Francisco preached twice as long as the average minister, and did it six times a week, plus whatever talks could be sandwiched in between. He did not lose as much weight as he did in New York, but his pace was one that no minister cared to imitate. Sacrifice, of course, is born of a sense of urgency, and issues in spiritual power. Years from now his real sacrifice will be known.

Billy Graham's humility has been the subject of many a discussion, and it is of a particularly disarming nature. There is a sense in which every man is a fortress, built by his own hands to protect his manhood. Many men pretend they have no fortress, but in the hour of insecurity their guard comes up. Billy Graham not only seems to have no fortress, he apparently does not even feel the need of one. Although he is a human being with normal contemporary problems of tenseness and occasional insomnia, spiritually he is so relaxed that he can laugh at himself and enjoy it. The Achilles' heel of every preacher is his sermon; it is the one point at which his pride is most vulnerable. Graham's reaction, however, is that he cannot see that his own preaching has much to commend it, except as the Holy Spirit uses it. He is painfully aware of his limitations. There are times, of course, when every person chooses to disclaim and to refuse to take credit; with Billy Graham it is a habit like breathing.

Liberty is a quality that has its technical side and its psychological side. A man with good rote memory can swing his arms in the pulpit and appear to have liberty of delivery. Liberty also has its spiritual aspect, however, and there were nights in the Cow Palace when Billy did not feel the freedom that has made him, according to *Holiday Magazine*, the world's "greatest living orator." The fact that he did exercise liberty in presenting his messages, and did not seem to be restricted to memoranda even when preaching over television to scores of millions of people, explains a good deal about Billy Graham. Exactly what liberty is, how much of it is a gift of God, how much audience rapport, how much I.Q., how much physical presence, are matters that had better be left.

Finally, I would suggest that Billy's secret lies in his love. A cynical age finds it difficult to believe that a successful evangelist actually loves the people to whom he preaches. There are undoubtedly nights when Billy's love is worn thin by fatigue, and when it is crowded out by duty. Yet those who know him best are the first to declare that he maintains a loving and gracious attitude toward those with whom he deals, whoever they are. Billy Graham certainly has his faults, and there are times when his geniality and agreeableness are the despair of his associates, and when he makes promises he cannot fulfill; but whatever his mistakes, they always seem to be made out of loving impulses. It is not a simpering love he radiates toward his audiences, nor is it a starry-eyed, innocent love; it is a clean, strong, manly, earnest love, with the purity of *agape* and the warmth of *eros*. It is the love of Christ as every Christian shows it at some time; Billy Graham just seems to have a little more of it than the rest of us.

San Francisco has some unforgettable memories of Billy. There were his presentations of notables on the platform: among others, Evangelist Mordecai Ham, who led him to Christ twenty-three years earlier; Roy Rogers, the actor; singer Ethel Waters, who called him "my child"; Stuart Hamblen, Jim Vaus and Louis Zamperini, all converts of nine years' standing who met Christ at Graham's "canvas cathedral" in Los Angeles; Bishop James Pike, newly consecrated in the chair of the Episcopal diocese of California; Dr. Charles E. Fuller of the "Old-Fashioned Revival Hour." There was the night Billy was bowed in prayer at the Cow Palace and a subpoena was dropped in his lap, ordering him to testify at a legislative committee hearing investigating pornography ... the wet, dripping noontime rally in Union Square ... the crowded City Hall plaza in Oakland ... the hot afternoon at San Quentin penitentiary, with over six hundred men responding to the challenge ... the night a key television cameraman fainted and the Cow Palace suddenly came alive with trotting ushers, and Billy never dropped a syllable ...

To those privileged to know him more intimately one memory that stands out is of Graham at prayer. De Rougemont suggests that man is most lucid when he prays, and it is certain that all of Graham's big decisions are forged in prayer. His times of intercession with the executive committee and team were high moments in the Crusade. The evangelist's prayers were the essence of simplicity. The Rev. Bill Rose, church editor of the Oakland *Tribune*, went to the Villa Motor Hotel to see Graham and after some time together, they knelt to pray. "I felt," said Rose, "as though I were praying with my own child." Even the evangelist's severest critics—and many of them are to be found within the Church—recognize the uniqueness of his spiritual nature.

In summary, it is not too much to suggest that the memory that will linger longest in the San Francisco area is simply the man himself. As Miss Rajkumari Amrit Kaur, member of India's Parliament and former minister of health, once expressed it, "Billy Graham is one of those rare jewels who tread this earth periodically and, by their lives and teaching, draw millions of others closer to God."

CHAPTER III · THE WORK AND THE WORKERS

The scope of the San Francisco Bay Cities Crusade was so broad, involving so many people and such diversified activity, that I have found it impossible to encompass it within a small book. Billy Graham was only one man, and there were many who labored together with him in a common effort to reach the community. Directing it all were the executive committee and the key men and women who made up the team. The Graham organization is a unique one, and some of its functions come to light in the stories that follow; a bare description must suffice for the rest.

Mass evangelism is not new to the American scene; it has found fertile soil in our country, and by the same token it has reaped a whirlwind of criticism. Indeed, by the time Billy Graham's Crusades were winning national attention, a large segment of the Church had discarded the techniques of mass evangelism altogether, and had consigned it to the limbo of history along with frontier revivals. New terms were in vogue: "visitation evangelism," "fellowship evangelism," "friendship calling" and "religious census." The common criticisms of mass evangelism—impermanence, exploitation, disorderliness, emotionalism—are still valid, for unfortunately the abuses are still with us.

The Graham Crusades have made their way, therefore, in the face of stubborn resistance on the part of some churches. If Graham's efforts have succeeded where others have failed it is because of two important discoveries on the part of the evangelist and his team: first, that the sins of mass evangelism are mostly sins of carelessness, and can be corrected by prudent supervision; and second, that mass evangelism is not the be-all and end-all of the Gospel, but only one arm of the Church's ministry.

These discoveries have led the team to do some remarkable pioneering along lines which have broken down resistance and have opened up new opportunities for the spreading of the Gospel. San Francisco followed the lead of New York in linking the Cow Palace meetings to an area-wide visitation evangelism project involving some three hundred churches during the week after the final meeting. According to the reports turned in by the churches, a total of 18,000 calls were completed by over 6,000 callers, and of those who were called on, 6,105 indicated "a definite desire to come to church."

As pastor of a participating church, I can give a personal testimony. I had wanted to conduct such a visitation for three years, but never got to it until the mass effort was arranged by the Crusade. Twenty-six people from our church went calling that week, and derived great joy and benefit from it. Thanks to the atmosphere created by the Crusade, the calls were spiritual and decision cards were used. Several families called upon came into the life of the Church, and a permanent visitation program was set up.

Not only did the Crusade seek to collaborate with other forms of evangelism, it brought a new emphasis on Bible teaching into the churches. For months after the Cow Palace meetings ended, the Crusade office remained open in San Francisco, not only to process pastors' referral cards but to train pastors and laymen in ways of establishing a simple, effective system of group Bible study.

One could wish for space to tell of the various achievements of the Crusade: the prayer ministry that proved such a blessing to hundreds of little neighborhood cell groups, breaking down spiritual barriers and reaching across denominational lines; the tremendous Saturday night telecasts that were double the size of New York's, extending into Canada for the first time and involving some 175 stations coast-to-coast; the "Operation Andrew" bus plan which was used by the churches to bring their non-Christian friends to the Cow Palace, as Andrew brought his brother Peter (John 1:41-42); the breakfast "workshops" for pastors in the Sheraton Palace Hotel, where the ministers' sights were raised and their Biblical theology sharpened; the work of the executive committee that caused Graham to comment that "this is the smoothest Crusade we have ever had"; the ministry to women's groups around the Bay; the work with university students; the prayer groups in stores, offices and institutions, and the work of Rev. George Bostrom in arranging pastors' prayer groups; the raising of the $400,000 budget by Lowell Berry, Mrs. William Lister Rogers and their committee; the telephone counseling ministry following the popular local television program, "Crusade Report"; the training of counselors, ushers and choir, and the background and preparation of it all.

It must suffice if certain personalities who served in key roles are mentioned and described in brief.

First on the list, even though she never appeared in San Francisco, is the lady whose part in the shaping of her husband's ministry can never be overestimated: Mrs. Ruth Bell Graham. It was the first major Crusade that she had to miss altogether, and there is a story behind her decision not to come that tells something of the kind of people with whom we are dealing. Mrs. Graham's family and friends had urged her to fly west for the final week before the mass meeting in Seals Stadium. Her husband and the team were to be vacationing in Monterey. With four children at home, including a fifteen-week-old infant, she had misgivings, but she took up the matter in prayer. The answer she gave her friends was: "If you can arrange a normal flight for me, booked straight through both ways, without using my name or hinting who it is, I'll go." The report came back that there were two sections of the flight for which no seats were available. "That settles it; I'm staying home," she announced. Her father, Dr. Nelson Bell, protested that if she would only let him, he could arrange a plane seat for her in a hurry. "No," she replied, "I have put out my fleece[1] and I have my answer."

[1] Judg. 6:37-40.

George Beverly Shea, the well-known soloist of the team, played a unique role in the meetings. He sang much and talked but little, yet his contribution to the spirit of the Crusade was such that it would be hard to think of its being held without him. "Bev" did not sing to entertain but to establish a mood; to calm the winds and the waves and to prepare hearts for receptivity to the Gospel. His vibrant baritone was only one of the weapons in his quiver; he spent much of his time on the platform in prayer. He was ably augmented by Ray Robles an American of Mexican ancestry, an acquisition of the Central American tour, whose melodious tenor was equally acceptable in Spanish or English.

The Rev. Walter H. Smyth, a former United Presbyterian minister from Bethesda, Maryland, was promoted from the oversight of group reservations at the New York Crusade to director in charge at San Francisco. It was a ten-month task and he acquired along the way a large office staff and an even larger crew of volunteer workers. One of his major undertakings was the setting up of committee personnel, and his other activities were multitudinous, not forgetting the financial side. He combined executive ability with a warm personality and ran his Crusade well. Immediately after the Seals Stadium meeting he left for Australia to take charge of preparations at Melbourne.

The Rev. Clifford Barrows, master of ceremonies, worship and song leader, trombonist, choir director, television program director and song-book editor, is probably the best-known member of the team apart from Graham himself. His personality and work are described elsewhere in this volume.

Tedd Smith, pianist, was joined in San Francisco by Lorin Whitney of the "Haven of Rest" program, who replaced Paul Mickelson at the organ. Their music was subdued and harmonious, and served the popular taste of Christians rather than attempting to scale the heights. They, too, were creating a mood for the Crusade.

Six associate evangelists assisted Dr. Graham in the actual ministry of the Gospel. They were the Rev. Grady Wilson, long-time friend and colleague who was won to Christ on the same night that Graham made his decision, twenty-three years before; the Rev. Joseph Blinco, of the Methodist Church of Great Britain, on loan to the United States; the Rev. Howard Jones of Cleveland, Ohio, an American Negro pastor who has conducted extensive evangelistic campaigns in West Africa; the Rev. Akbar Abdul Haqq, president of the Henry Martyn School of Islamics in New Delhi, India; the Rev. Leighton Ford, minister of the Presbyterian Church of Canada and brother-in-law of Graham, who at twenty-six years of age is already an established evangelist of international note; and the Rev. Ralph Mitchell, a veteran British evangelist of Scottish origin.

So brilliant are these men, so greatly sought after each in his own right, that it is difficult to conceive of them serving together as subluminaries on someone else's "team." The Bay Area soon discovered their speaking abilities, and kept them busy in churches, home meetings and conferences when they could be spared. Their caliber is indicative of Graham's gift for attracting effective men to his organization; or as he would term it, they are a manifestation of the leading of the Lord.

The Rev. Jerry Beavan, executive secretary to Graham and press relations adviser, who laid much of the groundwork in the early stages of the Crusade, left before the meetings began to arrange the 1959 Crusades in Melbourne and Sydney, Australia.

Mrs. Betty Lowry, in charge of the press department, quickly created a good working relationship with the Bay Area press. After she was taken ill, her position was filled by Miss Sarah Jepson, office manager at the 207 Powell Street headquarters and a valued member of the organization.

Charles Riggs served as director of the counseling program, as well as the follow-up work. With his colleague, Lorne Sanny, president of the Navigators, he conducted training classes for some 4,300 counselors in seven areas around the Bay, and labored diligently to bring their work —which was under constant scrutiny from the public— to a new level of efficiency. Their earnestness and thoroughness commended the program to pastor and layman alike. Robert Root and Dr. Charles Farah, also on loan from the Navigators, were key assistants, and maintained the follow-up office long after the Crusade had ended. Dr. Farah's staff of volunteers corrected Bible lessons, processed pastors' referrals and reassigned neglected inquiry cards until late in the fall.

Miss Patricia Campion, Miss Beryl Gilbertson, and Miss Myrl Flood, Christian young ladies of considerable poise and charm, represented the Crusade in its ministry to women and to the people of society. Miss Campion, a former actress, and Miss Gilbertson were both converts of the London Crusade.

Warner Hutchinson, a Phi Beta Kappa graduate of the University of California at Los Angeles and former navy chaplain, was assigned the task of carrying the Crusade to university students. When he was not arranging delegations to visit the Cow Palace, he was speaking and working with student groups on the various Bay Area campuses.

Bill Brown, assistant Crusade director, worked with chairman Oscar Schmaelzle to marshal a corps of several hundred ushers, whose task was to seat nearly 700,000 persons attending the Cow Palace meetings, as well as the 38,000 at the Seals Stadium finale. With Brown in San Francisco was his wife, the former Joan Winmill, British actress who appeared in the Graham film *Souls in Conflict*, based on the London Crusade.

The Rev. Willis Haymaker, one-time associate of Evangelist Billy Sunday, was in charge of arrangements for the 1,200 cottage prayer meetings that helped to prepare the area spiritually for the Crusade, and co-ordinated correspondence from 109 countries telling of prayers that were being offered for San Francisco.

Walter F. Bennett and Fred Dienert of the Walter F. Bennett Advertising Agency of Chicago, which handles the account of the Billy Graham Evangelistic Association, were on hand to oversee the detailed business arrangements of the Crusade.

One reason why the San Francisco meetings moved so well was the help of devoted local pastors. Full credit could never be properly assigned, but a few names will bear mentioning because of the unusual support that the ministers gave to the Crusade:

The Rev. Robert Boyd Munger, chairman of the ministers' advisory committee; the Rev. George Bostrom, chairman of the prayer committee; the Rev. Donald F. Lehmann, secretary of the executive committee and director of the telephone counseling ministry; the Rev. Ross F. Hidy, chairman of visitation evangelism; the Rev. Ernest L. Hastings, chairman of follow-up work; and the Rev. Sandford Fleming, chairman of the general Crusade Committee, were men who made outstanding contributions. They served under the leadership of two distinguished clergymen who acted as co-chairmen of the Crusade, the Rev. W. Earle Smith, executive of the Bay Cities Baptist Union, and the Rev. Carl G. Howie, pastor of Calvary Presbyterian Church, San Francisco. There were many, many others, clerical and lay, who gave unstintingly of time and energy to the Crusade effort.

Enough has been said to indicate the nature of the problem and the type of activity under consideration. The pages that follow will proceed to a closer examination of the Crusade. Individual lives, chosen for their representative nature, will be described as they came within the orbit of the Cow Palace meetings. Not all are "success stories," and not all have happy endings. All are essentially true and are based on actual experience, but in most cases names and places have had to be disguised for obvious reasons. Permission has been granted to use the stories, and it is hoped that they will tell better than any other kind of report, exactly what transpired at the San Francisco Bay Cities Crusade.

CHAPTER IV · THE PEOPLE

1. A STORY THAT NEVER MADE
THE CHURCH PAGE

So the Great Man was coming to town to hold a Crusade. Well, Alice Stephanian had lived through everything else, and she could live through this. Mr. Billy Graham would get the same kind of coverage on her page that she gave to all shouters and offering-takers. She knew the type, for she had been around. She had heard gentlemen—and ladies, too—claim all kinds of things as from the Lord. It was part of the day's work for the chic young church editor of the *Times*, San Francisco's self-styled "leading newspaper." For example, there was the chap who hired people to come to his tent meetings pretending to be deaf and dumb, and behold! suddenly they were cured. The police got that boy. Then there was the mesmerizer who put his whole audience into such a trance that Alice had to leave.

Thank God she, Alice Stephanian, had dropped anchor at last in a dignified, worshipful church from which she could look down upon all ninety-day-wonders and peg them for what they were. It had been quite a pilgrimage. She thought of her early years in the Armenian Orthodox Church, when her family made it a point to attend services regularly every Easter—and invariably arrived ten minutes late. She thought of the time when she was asked to be public relations director for a Council of Churches, only to have someone protest that she was of another faith. What was she, anyway?

Well, that was settled. It did not take the Lord long to lead Alice into the orbit of a number of devoted Christian workers who were associated with the Council of Churches. She was deeply impressed with the Council's program: the social work, the centers for senior citizens, the marriage counseling, the youth guidance activities, all capably staffed and functioning. Then one of the laywomen began to speak to Alice of spiritual things, of God, and faith, and Jesus Christ. She was deeply moved; no one else had ever talked with her thus. She began to attend her friend's church down the peninsula, and in due time received instruction. On June 2, 1957, seven years after she entered church work, Alice was confirmed in the beautiful Church of the Epiphany. In her *Book of Common Prayer* Alice's friend wrote, "This book and your faith will come to mean more to you."

For some weeks now the Graham press releases had been coming across her desk—in fact, ever since she had returned to it. Only two months earlier the *Times* had managed to woo her back from the Council of Churches to cope with the rising interest in religion. "We want this new Church Section to be different," the editors told her. "We want it to have a genuine ministry of its own, to have special features, to encourage the life of the churches." Alice had responded by getting out a precedent-shattering Easter edition of ten pages.

Billy Graham was arriving from Los Angeles on Saturday, it seemed, and a press conference was scheduled for nine o'clock at the Hotel Californian. Alice made it a point to be present, but on her guard. Everyone sat drinking coffee until Billy was introduced by the Crusade chairman. He seemed friendly and informal enough, and certainly gracious.

Then he began to speak of his reasons for coming. He said that he had not presumed to come to reform San Francisco . . . that he came because he and the team had been invited by the churches . . . that they hoped to make the Bay Area more conscious of its need for God . . . that no area outside of New York was more strategic for America than the Bay Area . . . that the whole nation needs an awakening, and it might well start here; in fact, fifty years ago Bishop Warren Candler of the Methodist Episcopal Church had predicted that it would . . . that Nehru had told Mrs. Adela Rogers St. John that Americans are selling the wrong things . . . that India wanted moral and spiritual qualities and did America have those qualities? . . . that he was not preaching sectarianism and was not trying to make Baptists of everybody . . . that the basic problem was not the H-bomb or the missile but the human heart.

Within five minutes Alice Stephanian had become a Graham admirer.

Sunday afternoon came and the Crusade opened in the Cow Palace as scheduled. Alice sat in the press box, thrilled at the size of the overflow crowd, and the fact that they were gathered for the cause of Jesus Christ. The preliminaries interested her. She watched Cliff Barrows chatting with his enormous choir over the mike as though they were twenty out for Thursday night rehearsal, leading them in his shirt sleeves through the strains of "How Great Thou Art." She noted the quiet arranging of counselors in strategic places near the front, the boxes for special guests, the cripples being wheeled in, the section for the deaf. Now a lady in an iron lung was being lifted from a truck equipped with a special generator. No one was smoking. No one was drinking. Crowds were streaming into the highest corners, and ushers were everywhere. Now the huge overhead lights flashed on and the pleasant murmur of voices increased. Flash camera fans were marshaled along the corridor where Billy Graham was expected to appear. Cliff and the choir had finished rehearsing, and he had slipped out. Bill Brown was giving the choir some seating instructions, for the crowd was pressing into their section. He told them that the traffic was backed up six miles along the Bayshore Freeway. The platform guests took their seats—the executive committee fresh from its prayer meeting, together with the municipal dignitaries.

Suddenly the choir stood up and Cliff Barrows, fully suited, was leading over 1,500 voices in "This is my Story, this is my Song, praising my Savior all the day long." Flash bulbs were popping; Dr. Graham had slipped quietly onto the platform. The Crusade had begun . . .

In a few moments Billy was preaching his first sermon, and as Alice listened, she found herself hearing no man at all, but rather a message. She seemed to be talking to her

68

own heart, telling herself things she had always known, yet had she ever known them? Being a church editor, she thought, is not exactly the same as being a Christian. Why did that seem such a new idea? The truth was that in her eight years in the field Alice had acquired a great deal of information about the ways in which people worship God, but not too much about God Himself. Something was missing, and this afternoon that something seemed to be just about the most important thing of all.

Gathering information had always been Alice's forte. Since she was a fourteen-year-old schoolgirl at Richmond High, she had wanted to go to work for the *Times*. After two years at City College of San Francisco she had achieved her goal, but she had started at the bottom—a classified ad telephone girl. One day they asked her if she would consider writing the church page. The incumbent had just been sacked and she knew it. Furthermore she knew that no one wanted the job. The church page ranked in popularity around the *Times* with the obituary column; but when you're at the bottom, where can you go but up? Alice took the job.

The information was collected and the notices were written, and she made plenty of mistakes. She called the ministers "Father" and the priests "Mister." She made history by describing the Hindu Vedanta Society as "The Vendetta Society." But she stuck with it and she won. Only now, as she sat in the Cow Palace on that first Sunday afternoon, was she becoming aware that there was still a deep emptiness in her life. *To know God*, she thought. *To know that Someone is talking to me. That I am being spoken to. To know this . . .*

Midway through the Crusade Alice found herself having a difficult week both professionally and personally.

She thought of the comfort she had found in her Prayer Book, and how Christians in such emergencies had learned always to turn to the Lord. She decided that nothing would keep her from the Cow Palace on that particular evening.

It was Thursday, one of the fabulous Thursday nights when the Cow Palace was filled to capacity, mostly with teenagers. Billy Graham was in his element. He mentioned the young man who went to church and told the pastor at the door, "Dad, you really blasted me this morning. That sermon was neat and really sweet and you were on the beam, Dad. You were cool, I mean real cool, Dad." And the minister gulped and said with astonishment, "I beg your pardon." The teen-ager continued, "Dad, I mean you were really on the beam, I was reading you clear. That jive was so hepped that I dropped twenty simolas in the plate. Dad, you were great." And the minister smiled and said, "Crazy, man, cra-a-zy." Then Billy preached a colorful Bible message about David and Goliath. He spoke of the "giants in our lives" and how they can be overcome with the pebbles of faith.

Alice returned home amazed at how refreshed she felt. The next day each problem seemed to fit into its solution and order was re-established. She found herself in a pliable mood; her attitudes had softened, and even more important, she sensed that she was not alone. From that day she attended the Crusade faithfully each evening until the closing meeting in the Cow Palace on a Sunday afternoon in mid-June.

The press box was on the main floor, at the left of the choir. Alice sat between two colleagues looking out for the last time at the giant crowd. Tomorrow night the cigar butts would return and the bars would reopen. Tomorrow night the huge sign, "I AM THE WAY, THE TRUTH AND THE LIFE" would be taken down. Tomorrow night there would be a boxing match and the air would be blue. There would be no thousand tongues to sing the Great Redeemer's praise.

Alice tried to evaluate the tall young evangelist and what his Crusade had done for her city. She thought of the barbs of ridicule, the honest criticisms and the misunderstandings she had listened to. She thought of the thousands of youths who had choked the aisles clear to the back of the auditorium in their eagerness to dedicate their lives to Jesus Christ. She remembered the expressions on their faces.

Then she thought of her own life: the commandments she had broken, the things she had done that she was not proud of. She realized how hollow her life was without Jesus, how rich it was with Him. She had learned from Billy about "arrow-point prayers," and she sent up one now to God. Was this the time? She did want solace, serenity, satisfaction; yet how could she take a public stand? What would people say—the people she worked with, whose co-operation provided her daily bread? What would her co-workers of the press say? "My, Miss Stephanian, you make a fine actress!"

The sermon ended in a final appeal for commitment. Alice knew that she was being invited to let the good Lord come into her life. Next to her was her friend Betty Cooper of the Berkeley *Gazette*, who had given her a Bible. Betty's eyes were closed as she turned to look. She realized her prayer had been answered: she would give herself to Jesus Christ. The choir was humming as Alice Stephanian, church editor of the San Francisco *Times*, rose and stepped into the open space before the press box.

Within a few moments Alice was in the counseling room, while back at the press table typewriter keys were clicking out the wrap-up:

It is Sunday afternoon in the Cow Palace. The last strains of the closing doxology have just died away, and from the press table there is unfolding an unforgettable sight. Thousands of people are gathered in little clusters, talking, laughing, not a few weeping. After seven weeks, the Billy Graham San Francisco Bay Cities Crusade is ended. Only the final rally in Seals Stadium remains. The Crusade choir, two thousand strong, has just sung "How Great Thou Art!" for the last time in this giant stock-show arena which for the past seven weeks has been a cathedral of the Holy Spirit.

The rostrum where only a few minutes ago the evangelist was proclaiming saving truth is now empty, save for a single small boy who is looking for his mother. In the corridors the autograph hunters and flash-camera fans are relentlessly stalking their quarry. In an exhibit room at the right nearly a thousand inquirers have confessed their sins in a simple prayer, and are now being shown by their counselors how to fill out the answer to the first question in their first Bible lesson: "Why was the Gospel of John written?"

No one can believe that it is over.

But for Alice Stephanian, as for thousands of others who were walking in newness of life, it wasn't over at all. It was just beginning.

2. ACROSS THE STREET TO HEAVEN

It could have happened while gunner Fred Hadley was parachuting to earth from a flaming B-17 over the Nazi submarine base at Nantes on September 16, 1943. Certainly many another young soldier had prayed in such a strait. Or it could have happened during the two years he spent in

Stalag 17, along with seventeen hundred other prisoners from the States. There were chaplains and services and prayer cells behind the barbed wire; but Fred Hadley left them strictly alone.

Nothing happened, in fact, until the year 1957, by which time Fred was a high-pressure food salesman, had a wife and three lovely children, and lived in a suburban home near San Francisco. God chose a most undramatic circumstance to make His entrance into Fred's life: an assist from a neighbor in moving some furniture. The man did not move the stuff with any special dexterity, nor did he make a display of wit or wisdom. He simply seemed to be different. As Fred remarked that evening to his wife Roberta, he had never seen a man wearing such a peaceful look.

"How does he get that way? What's his gimmick? I never saw the tranquilizer that could produce that effect." But all his investigation yielded was that the man was an elder in the church that the Hadleys infrequently attended. Go-getter Fred promptly decided to institute a search. He began attending church more regularly and studying the faces of the worshipers, sorting out the members who had "that look." He decided there were not very many, but he kept his conclusions to himself, while his pastor talked him into attending a membership training class. Within a few weeks he completed the course and appeared before the church board where he made the usual profession of faith in Jesus Christ. "Boy," thought Fred Hadley, "how I am fooling these people. To think anyone could pick up the social prestige of membership in this church so easily."

But Fred's church was not a casual church, and its pastor was not one to minimize the claims of Christ on a man's life. Before three months had passed the new member was saying a prayer before going to bed. It was the prayer of a salesman, and it read like an order blank; Fred reflected his vocation. His petitions before the Almighty were independent, self-centered and shrewd, and aimed at a calculated effect. They were the soliloquies of a man who in past years had looked at death full in the face and had never once thought of God. Given a few more years of exposure to Christian doctrine and Fred might have gathered what it was about; as it was, he was fitting all too typically into the role of Mr. Average Church Member.

Late in April, 1958, a sales conference was set up, to be held high in the company's office building in San Francisco, and the docket was duly promulgated. A little after five o'clock, as was the custom, the meeting adjourned; and as was the custom, the salesmen agreed to go somewhere for a little drink.

"Which shall it be?" asked one.

"How about the Players Club?" suggested another, and the others nodded and walked to their cars.

The Players Club is a bar located just south of the boundary line of San Francisco, near the western shore of the Bay. It caters heavily to the sports and stock enthusiasts who frequent the Cow Palace opposite. Within a few moments half a dozen salesmen had walked through the magic glass doors and had lined up at the club's altar in ritualistic fashion.

"This one's on me," intoned the end man, and the others murmured protestingly and then barked their orders. Fred Hadley took his Scotch and soda and leaned against the bar as he gazed abstractedly through the glass doors at the street. Conscience? Not a bit of it. This was how the world lived, and he could tick you off plenty of members of his church who did the same thing. Some didn't—like the

74

neighboring elder—but Fred was only a social drinker anyway.

"Look at the mob, would you," commented Al beside him, indicating the street with his glass.

"Where are they all going?" asked Fred.

"Oh, you know, the Billy Graham business over there."

"Mmm."

Only a few nights before Fred and Roberta had talked about Billy Graham. They had agreed it would be nice to try to take him in while he was in town. But what with one thing and another . . .

It was time for the second movement of the ritual, and Al lifted his voice in incantation. "This round's on me." Again the quiet murmurs of approval as the libations were poured; but Fred began to feel uneasy. The crowd was moving more swiftly now, and something seemed to be drawing him through those glass doors. He took a long pull and fought it off, but it returned. He spoke in a low voice to Al: "Why don't we go over and hear what he's got to say?"

Al turned away from the television. "Are you crazy? The fights are coming on at seven." He looked at his watch and turned back to his program. "Wait till after that, and I dunno—I might go with you."

Fred stared at his half-finished drink, and a new thought struck a chill through him. The third round of drinks would be on him; it was his priestly turn at the altar. His hand trembled as he reached for his wallet and surreptitiously examined it. Two one-dollar bills! He pushed back his glass and waved to the others nonchalantly.

"Think I'll go across the street and see what's doing. See you fellows later."

They did not bother to interrupt their conversations;

they couldn't have cared less. Just as long as a third round was set up by someone, let's see, whose . . . ?

The wind was blowing, and Fred was quickly lost in the hurrying crowd, as sixteen thousand streamed toward the arena, and all but he seemed to know where they were going. Most of them clutched tickets. He joined a waiting mass before the main doors, but within a few moments they were swung open and Fred went in with the surge, found a seat at the back, and sat down.

As a prisoner of war Hadley had learned not to rely too heavily on human statements. (For six months he was reported simply "Missing in Action.") As a salesman he knew how to estimate the value of words; furthermore he was born in Texas, which is not far from Missouri. But that night as he listened to Billy Graham preach a straight gospel in strong words, Fred felt that the man's message was built right around his own life. It was a letter addressed to him personally—to Fred Hadley, fugitive from the Lord. About halfway through the sermon odd things began to happen— Fred's heart began to thump and knots formed in his stomach. "I'm having a heart attack," he thought. He looked up at the huge ceiling with its girders and catwalks, and began to pray, and as he prayed it became clear to him what was taking place. He felt the Presence of the living God. The love of Christ, he saw, was something completely different from what he had imagined it to be. He had never conceived of anyone doing anything for him, never thought of the Cross of Jesus Christ as meaning anything in his own life.

Now Billy was giving an invitation, urging people to come forward, and Fred had never dreamed of this either; yet his heart was pounding, telling him he ought to. He couldn't! The uneasy feeling became more intense. He stood up, the tears streaming down his cheeks, and moved toward the rostrum.

It was nearly midnight when Fred arrrived home to find a waiting and anxious wife. He had already had a hard time trying to explain to a counselor why he had come forward, and as he talked to his wife she was even more mystified. Fred gave up and went to bed, not to sleep, but to pray, doze, and pray until daylight. After breakfast, it being Saturday, he went to see his minister, who promptly asked him to give a testimony the next day.

There are three children in the Hadley home: a daughter, Melanie, aged eleven, and two smaller ones, James and Sally. That evening Fred was back in the Cow Palace with Melanie. While she listened to the Gospel, Fred tried to "can" a speech he could give the next morning to the members of his church. Melanie responded to Dr. Graham's message with her first decision for Jesus Christ, and Fred was delighted, but back home he spent another restless night. In the morning he went to church early and hunted up the prayer room off the sanctuary, for by this time he was frightened. During his fervent prayer the Lord gave him peace; and a short while later, before seven hundred people, Fred Hadley made his confession of faith. He had joined the people of "that look."

Later that day Fred had cause to remember a phrase Billy Graham had used the night before: "When you receive Jesus Christ, don't look for all your problems to be solved. They may be increased, because now you are taking a stand for Him." Fred remembered because his first Sunday as a Christian was not a particularly happy one. The salesman's hardest prospects are his own kinfolk; and his wife Roberta was not about to be sold. What Fred wanted to do with his life was his own business, but her faith was a private matter. She had been brought up in a church in Spokane, had thought things through on her own, and she did not need Billy Graham to tell her what to believe. Furthermore, she did not intend to give up her social drinking.

That night Salesman Hadley dreamed that he was with some people who were serving soup to a crowd which did not care too much for it. Then someone added an ingredient to the soup, and everyone began to clamor for it. They were informed, however, that the price of the soup had risen to two thousand dollars a bowl, and they turned away, and Fred awoke, wondering how to interpret his dream. The "new ingredient," he believed, was the blood of Jesus Christ.

During the week Fred set out to rectify some wrongs. First he called on Ralph and Barbara, and it took a bit of doing, for he had quit a former job with another firm simply because Ralph got on his nerves. Ralph was away at work when Fred called at the home, and Barbara was speechless with astonishment as she saw him in the doorway. What on earth . . . ?

"I have some tickets here for the Cow Palace," said Fred, "I thought if you and Ralph would like to go, I'd call for you."

"Just—just a minute, I'll call him," stammered Barbara. She dialed the number and relayed the message, and there was a shocked silence on the line, then a negative response punctuated with expletives.

Later that day Fred was driving past their house, saw Barbara out front, and waved. She beckoned to him: "Ralph called back an hour later and said he's decided he'd like to go."

That night Ralph and Barbara went forward at the Crusade and friendship was re-formed on a new level.

Fred began to organize trips to the Cow Palace for nearly every night. He took some people who received little help; yet eighteen of his passengers (including his wife's mother) responded to the invitation and made some kind of decision. At the same time things were not going well at home; relationships were deteriorating, and Fred felt his dream was being acted out, and that two thousand dollars apparently was still too high for a bowl of soup. Roberta, however, pointed out that it wasn't the first time he had gone into something head-over-heels.

"You always do things quickly and emotionally," she told him.

"Can I help it?" he wanted to know.

"No, but I can."

"Do what you like. All I know is, Christ has become real to me for the first time, and I am not going to give up what I have found, no matter what."

"Nobody's asking you to give it up, but why do you have to upset everything? Why do you have to try to change my pattern of life too?"

There came an evening when Roberta agreed to go to the Cow Palace. She sat quietly, listened, said nothing, and when the invitation was given she made no move. As they drove home they discussed the sermon calmly and rather thoughtfully.

"Just what is it you think you have found?" she asked.

"I don't know. It's hard to put into words. I just feel that Christ is with me."

"I noticed you reading the Bible late last night."

"That's part of it. I never in my life spent half an hour in the Bible, and now I can hardly put it down."

"Do you think it will wear off?"

"I don't know. I never had anything like this before. But the pastor has asked me to head up the new visitation campaign, and I guess that will keep me on the ball for awhile."

"It's nice what you did for Ralph and Barbara."

"Thanks."

Two days later Roberta asked if she could go to the Cow Palace again. Fred was delighted. He did not hear the sermon very clearly owing to his inward excitement, but when Billy Graham appealed to his audience to receive Jesus Christ, Fred bowed his head as Roberta rose in quiet dignity and walked to the front.

After she was seated in a room adjoining, Roberta's counselor asked her, "Why did you make a decision tonight?"

Roberta answered slowly and reflectively, "Ever since my husband came here, I have been asking myself whether I have been missing something. Tonight I found the answer. I have lost sight of Christ, and I want Him back."

As she came out of the counseling room Fred was there waiting, with a rueful smile on his face; he knew how hard he had made it for her. He knew why she had resisted the thing that had happened to him. He knew there would still be problems—his impetuosity, his irritability. And next month there would be another sales meeting. But as she emerged, all problems at the moment seemed to be suspended; for she had on her face a look—a look of peace . . .

3. PARALLEL LINES MEET AT INFINITY

Somewhere out on the high seas as I write these words is Chief Steward Harry Eckerman, fighting the battle of his life. For some alcoholics the change-over to a life in Christ has been instantaneous, complete and permanent. For Harry it will always be a battle, but it is now God's battle too. To see a spark of will power come into this drenched, sodden personality is to behold Lazarus newly emerged in all his grave wrappings. No one knows how long Lazarus lived after he revived, and no one knows how long Harry will "last." To listen to his wife Sylvia, whose life he has made a liquid hell for six years, one would say—

But let us not say anything. Let us just observe.

Walk with me along Drumm Street, past the Seamen's Hiring Hall, past the Scandinavian Seamen's Home. Here is the fertile breeding ground of the lush and the "wino." Here San Francisco multiplies its statistics in the field of alcohol. As you walk, note the prostrate figure that you step over. He lies sprawled athwart the sidewalk, attired in the shabby jeans and greasy coat of an unemployed seaman. This is Harry Eckerman. His face is weather-creased and his glass eye is staring. Around his lips the mushy flesh shows through his beard and betrays the confirmed alcoholic. You need not shake your head; such sights are common enough in the City by the Golden Gate.

Now the body is stirring and beginning to moan. Harry seeks to lift his head from the curb and falls back with an oath. The pain is evidently in his hip; he tries again, and after an interminable period gets to his feet. Propped against the wall, he drags his leg a few yards before collapsing again. Half an hour later he manages to pull himself into the shabby little room where he has been living ever since the last time Sylvia closed the door of their home upon him.

Every other week Sylvia goes to the psychiatrist who, she says, has saved her from insanity. She pays him seventy-five cents an hour because that is all that can be spared from her tiny baby-sitting income, and because he is kind. The little flat that she maintains in the Mission district is poor enough, but it has the dignity San Francisco loves to lend to its old establishments. Time after time she has thrown Harry out of the house because his wild excesses could no longer be endured. For two whole years he lived down by the Hiring Hall on Drumm Street, working and loafing ashore because his eye handicapped him when he applied for sea duty. He spent a Christmas in the Marine Hospital vomiting blood; another Christmas completely paralyzed on the right side; and inevitably he returned to the source of his ailments.

Two days after the fall on Drumm Street, Sylvia answered the telephone in her flat:

"It's me. Can I come home?"

"What's wrong?" (Something must be wrong; he was sober.)

"I got hurt, I don't know how. It's my hip."

"Where are you?"

"At the room. I can't stay here. They keep feeding me drinks."

Sylvia went down to get him. She was half an hour in the rooming house, and during that time on five different occasions there came a knock at the door. Each time it was a "wino" with a jug, seeking companionship.

Back in the flat in the Mission district, she put her husband to bed. She removed the filthy clothes, examined the battered and bruised hip, cleaned and shaved him and fed him black coffee. Then she looked at the man to whom she had been joined in marriage for six years. How does one evaluate a washed-up life? What yardstick does the psychometrist use? Harry Eckerman had been at sea since he was sixteen years old, when he joined the Navy as a fireman aboard the *USS Holland*. Thirty-four years of travel to the distant crannies of the world, promotion to chief steward, serving up meals aboard submarines deep in combat zones during World War II, a long and honorable record, and now—this.

The days went by and the hip slowly mended. Each afternoon Sylvia would leave Harry sitting on the little sofa and would walk the ten long blocks to the flat where she spent the next nine hours caring for the children of a working mother. As she walked she sifted her marriage for any possible grounds of hope. Harry was fifty years old. Can the leopard change his spots? Sylvia did not think so. Every voyage ended in a port, and every dry spell ended in a spree. Sylvia shook her head, and counted the days until she would see her psychiatrist.

That night, with her charges in bed, she turned on the television and discovered a new program on the air. A cheerful and enthusiastic young man was telling about the great things that were happening at the Cow Palace, where the evangelist Billy Graham was holding meetings. Sylvia wished she could go. Shattered as she was by the catastrophes that had rocked her life—and Harry was only one of them—there was a corner of her heart that said "Yes" to the things Billy was saying. Cliff Barrows' news report gave her vicarious satisfaction.

Suddenly she sat bolt upright, for on the screen Cliff was flashing a telephone number. "Just pick up your phone and call EXbrook 7-1242," he was saying. "There's a counselor standing by waiting to talk to you." She telephoned.

When she reached home late that night, a familiar smell pervaded the house. Harry had been out for supplies.

"Why didn't you come walk me home?" Her voice was shrill.

"Went to see a fellow owes me eighty dollars."

"Did you get it?"

"He's a funny guy. Said the only way he'd pay me was, I'd have to drink it up."

Sylvia thought about the telephone conversation and began to cry. "Maybe someone can help you if I can't. Maybe God can reach you, but I doubt it." She went to her room.

Some time earlier, with the encouragement of her psychiatrist, Sylvia had begun attending a local church. Once Harry had accompanied her; but it was not really his cup of tea. "Candy is dandy, but liquor is quicker." Sylvia found the people pleasant and she liked the minister who came to visit; but who could expect these folks to help clear away the rubble of her life? Even Alcoholics Anonymous had tried and failed. Now she had tried Billy Graham, and that outlet too seemed doomed; for some reason no counselor had come to call.

The telephone ministry of the Billy Graham Crusade was located in the Crusade offices on Powell Street in the heart of San Francisco. Each evening at ten-forty-five, after the telephone number had been flashed, the sixteen phones began ringing. Answering the phones were laymen and ministers skilled in this special method of counseling. They secured basic information; they listened and drew out the problem; they quoted relevant Scripture from an open Bible; they sought gently to lead the caller to a decision. Occasionally the inquirer was a crank or a prankster; usually those on the end of the line were intelligent and hard-pressed people.

Two weeks had gone by since Sylvia's first call, and once again drunkenness reigned in her home. Night after night she watched the Crusade Report on television, and prayed, and wondered. She thought that if she could get Harry to call in, he, perhaps, would get action. They might listen to a man. One afternoon as she left for her walk to work, she wrote out the name on a slip of paper and gave it to him. "Call it," she urged. Then that night she watched the tele-cast again, and when the number was flashed she could wait no longer. She telephoned a second time.

Meanwhile, back at the flat, Harry sat drinking. He grimaced as if he were taking poison, but he could not stop. Yet he knew that he could not continue much longer; his body could not take the strain. Sylvia had given him orders to leave. "I must do something," he thought. "God help me. I've got to break out of it." The television set blabbed on, but he hardly noticed it. "Got to break out . . . break out . . ." Suddenly a voice pierced his consciousness. "There's a counselor standing by waiting to talk to you. There's help for you at this number." Now the program was off the air, but he continued to stare unmovingly. What was that number? He had forgotten.

In the Crusade offices that night activities were drawing to a close. It had been a good evening; over seventy calls had come in. Now the telephones had stopped ringing. Most of the counselors had turned in their reports and had gone home, for sleep was precious these days. It was nearly ten-thirty, and Sue was ready to disconnect the switch-board when it suddenly came alive. "Here's a call, will someone take it?"

Ed Driscoll left his report and picked up the receiver. "Billy Graham Crusade, may I help you?"

The voice was muffled and unsteady. "I just found this number on a piece of paper—I guess my wife left it here."

"Yes. Could you tell me your name?"

"Eckerman, Harry Eckerman."

As Ed spelled it out another counselor whispered, "That's the name of the woman I just talked to a moment ago!" She went through the pile of evening reports swiftly, drew out the sheet in question, and laid it beside Ed. It read:

"Inquirer's Name: Mrs. Eckerman.

"Define Need: Behalf of husband, an alcoholic, but recognized her own need for salvation. She's desperate, trying to do all she can herself to keep him. Merchant seaman.

"Type of Decision: Acceptance of Christ."

Harry was speaking slowly over the telephone: "I don't know what to do. I figure God is the only one that can help me. Right now I'll grab at anything."

Gently, as on a foggy night the man at the control tower talks his plane safely to earth, Ed sought to talk his man into the Kingdom of God. A decision was made. A counseling appointment was set for the following afternoon. Driscoll took time from his work, called, and arranged to pick up the Eckermans Sunday and take them to the Cow Palace. When Sunday came, Harry was sober. And when Evangelist Billy Graham concluded his sermon, as he always does, with an invitation, Harry was the first one out of his seat. His wife watched open-mouthed as he half stumbled over the people seated next to him and walked down the aisle to the front of the auditorium. Whatever was on his mind? Was the nightmare actually going to end? Was the leopard going to change his spots? In her heart she prayed, but she told herself that Harry was only putting on an act to please her. Hadn't they told her at Napa State Hospital that he was a confirmed alcoholic? She had learned to steel herself against disappointment and disillusionment. Never again would she be trapped.

The next day Harry Eckerman got drunk.

In his classic South Seas story, *Rain*, Somerset Maugham tells of the experiences of the prostitute Sadie Thompson in the realm of religion. She meets a missionary who counsels her into a life of faith, only to succumb himself to her fleshly charms. Sadie ends as she began, more cynical than ever, and Mr. Maugham observes that human nature never really changes.

Yet Billy Graham had undoubtedly stirred something in Harry—something more than yeast. It was a frightful battle that he faced: Harry Eckerman against San Francisco. Harry Eckerman against the glass of death. Harry Eckerman against the flesh and its roaring. Harry Eckerman against the sorceress' potion that would turn him into a toad.

For Sylvia there was a battle, too, against cynicism and unbelief, against the resentments of the years. She tried to rejoice when she saw him cutting down on his liquor consumption, but it is hard to strike fire in cold ashes.

Harry prayed, read his Bible, went to the Hiring Hall and looked for work. His pals were there—delighted to see him, eager to ply him with drinks. Harry would counter with an invitation of his own: "Would you like to go out to the Cow Palace?" Meanwhile the outlook continued bleak and no work was to be had. Billy Graham preached his closing sermon. The people from the church received his referral card, and they called at the flat. Sylvia had joined the membership a year before; but Harry found the alcoholic's usual difficulty in making a church adjustment. Besides, it is hard for a man to fight when his hands are idle. It is hard to claim a victory in a land of living corpses—and that is all he had known.

One Saturday night on the Billy Graham telecast the whole nation learned that Harry and Sylvia had telephoned the Crusade offices for help on the same evening; but no jobs came forth. "Want a one-eyed alcoholic sailor who has just found Jesus Christ, anyone?"

On June 21, 1958, Chief Steward Harry Eckerman signed aboard a tramp freighter as an ordinary messman, taking a drop in rating to get the job. It was the first time he had ever been willing to do it. Sylvia was proud of him. If only someone would take an interest in him, she thought, he might yet—she dared not say it. She went down to the dock to wave good-by, and offered a prayer of hope as Harry shipped out to fight his battle.

4. SHIRLEY MOVES TO DALY CITY

The Rev. Montgomery Petrie looked at his watch as he walked up the stairs to the door of the apartment house. One-fifteen in the morning! An odd hour for an honest and rather sleepy clergyman to be about the streets of San Francisco. Had his wife not been ill, he would have insisted she come along. Even in the city famed for its nocturnal inclinations, he noticed that most of the windows were dark. How long had it been since he paid a call in the middle of the night, when there was no sickness except sickness of soul? It would be like this, he reflected, when revival came: men and women crying out for the living God, like this nineteen-year-old who had hauled him out of bed because she felt "awful" and had to talk. . . . He uttered a quick prayer, pushed the buzzer and smiled as the door opened.

"Good evening, Miss Plummer."

"Good evening, sir. Please come in." Shirley was an attractive brunette, dressed in San Francisco taste, and was apparently alone. She murmured apologies, offered him a chair, and come to the point: at one-thirty one does not beat around the bush.

"Mr. Petrie, how do I know whether I am saved?"

What should he do? Fire away out of the Book, or dig beneath her question to find out what conflict had brought it to the surface? He had read a book on "non-directive counseling"; but this girl had been coming to church for years. He decided a straight question deserved a straight answer.

"Salvation, Shirley, is a gift of God. We receive it when we commit our lives to Jesus Christ as our Savior and our Lord. 'But as many as received him, to them gave he power to become the sons of God, even to them that believe on his name.' Do you believe that?"

"How can I? I don't know what it means. How do you 'believe on his name?'"

"Well, it's an act of faith. Once you place your trust in Christ, He takes over your life and transforms it, and you are born of the Spirit."

"What does that mean?"

"It means that the power that was released when Jesus Christ sacrificed Himself upon the Cross is made available to you. You are washed and cleansed in His blood, and your sins are forgiven, and you are made whole."

"And that's salvation?"

"Yes. Of course it's only the beginning."

"Well, I thought I had been through all that."

"So did I, Shirley. I was rather surprised when you raised your hand and asked for prayer this morning."

"Sometimes, Mr. Petrie, people don't live the kind of lives their ministers think they do. When I went to the Billy Graham meeting the other night and he started talking about 'escapism,' I realized all of a sudden that that's exactly what I've been doing for years, running away from God."

"What did you do about it?"

Shirley shrugged her shoulders. "I didn't do anything. When he gave the invitation I felt I ought to go, but something held me back, and tonight I'm afraid I've done something wrong—rejected the Holy Ghost, perhaps—and I'm confused . . ."

Quietly and skillfully the minister talked peace into the heart of the girl. He spoke to her of the love of the heavenly Father; of the everlasting arms that were open to welcome and receive her. Gently he mentioned the forces loose in the world that sought to strike confusion in the mind of the believer; then he pointed to the wonder of God's forgiving Grace, that was able to overcome every obstacle and to claim her for His own. He went over two passages of the New Testament, John 3:16 and I Corinthians 10:13, until she seemed to understand.

"Do you believe now that you are saved?" he asked at last.

"Well," she hesitated, "I have asked God's pardon for my sins, but I don't feel that He has taken them all away."

"If you are still in doubt," suggested Mr. Petrie as he closed his Bible, "it may be that there is an area of your life that you have not been willing to lay on the altar of God."

It was nearly three o'clock when the pastor departed and

Shirley took her Bible and went to bed, but not to sleep. For two hours she flipped the pages back and forth, trying to find an answer that would bring comfort and poise. At five o'clock she snapped off the lamp and went to sleep, but an hour later she suddenly awoke, pulse throbbing, nerves tingling, an odd sensation in her throat. She knew at last what it was that she had to do. In the bright light of discovery she looked back over the years and wondered why it had taken her so long . . .

Eugene Plummer was not the easiest man in the world to live with. Raised in a Christian family and graduated from a church college in Idaho, he had wanted to become a minister himself, but life had led him into other paths—into pipe covering and boiler installation. He married a devout church girl, Mavis, whose father was a minister, and they had one daughter, Shirley, the joy and blessing of the home. Eugene had been a fighter at one time, and was apt to be forceful in his dealings with his wife and daughter. On the other hand he was of a generous nature and would help anyone even if it meant no extra groceries for the family. The result was financial difficulty and constant argument about bills. The usually quiet Eugene began to change under the pressure. One day in a fit of annoyance he shouted to Mavis, "If you would go to work, we could pay our bills. Why don't you go out and earn some money?"

Many times afterward Eugene was to swallow those words, but they had been uttered and it was too late. Mavis found bookkeeping work with a firm uptown, and during the day she turned nine-year-old Shirley over to baby-sitters. Life immediately began to open up new vistas for Mavis, as the people who employed her were congenial and took a liking to her. She was invited to join the company's bowling team, and began to spend her evenings among the convivial spirits of the bowling alley, with Shirley tagging along. A bar adjoined the alley, and soon modest Mavis was "living it up" and looking with pity and scorn at her former circumscribed existence as Mrs. Eugene Plummer. That man, she became convinced, was a fanatic on the subject of religion. How different were the folks in the bowling alley, and how relaxed it was amidst all the beer and the jolly folk.

It did not take long for Shirley to adapt herself to the program of emancipation. She, too, began to rebel at the strictness of her father and his church. At the bowling alley she became friendly with a boy whose name was Diego, and by the time she was fifteen years old they were "going steady." Eugene watched the trend of events with increasing disapproval, and tension mounted in the home. Soon the storm broke and Mavis packed her bags and moved uptown, taking Shirley with her; and instead of one home there were two.

The gay life of the city now entered Mavis' apartment and the parties were "fabulous." Occasionally Mavis was troubled by the fact that Shirley was being exposed to it all, and when she got a raise in salary she decided on a happy solution: she would rent still another apartment for social activities, and keep Shirley where she now was. So instead of two homes there were three. Right about this time Eugene found work slack in the region, and went to Los Angeles to take a temporary job. Shirley would come home from high school to spend nights at the apartment in desperate loneliness. She became terrified of sounds in the dark. Only her girl friends and the faithful Diego kept her from losing her senses; yet all of the time she remained loyal to her mother. When Eugene telephoned hopefully and invited Mavis and Shirley to go to church with him, Shirley relayed the flimsy excuses her mother invented, and defended them gladly.

On Good Friday of 1958, Shirley and her girl friend Terry attended a service at a suburban church on the peninsula, and noticed a Billy Graham announcement in the narthex as they left. Terry asked Shirley if she would like to go, and as a result on the first Wednesday evening of the Crusade the two girls drove to the Cow Palace . . .

At ten o'clock in the morning the telephone rang; it was Mr. Petrie, who had only left some seven hours before. "How do you feel today?" he asked.

"I feel wonderful," exclaimed Shirley, "and I'll never forget your kindness. My prayer got through, and I know what's got to be done."

After he had hung up, Shirley closed her eyes a moment and then dialed the number she knew so well—her mother's business firm.

"Hello, mother."

"Hello, dear."

"I'm going to leave, mother."

"What do you mean?" Mavis was panicked.

"I'm not going to stay. I'm going back to father. I'm tired of lying and I'm sick of your friends. I'm giving up Diego, too."

"But why?" Mavis could hardly believe her ears.

"I feel God wants me to."

Mavis rushed home and mother and daughter talked for five hours. Mavis made a number of promises: she would not bring her friends to the apartment again; she would go to church; she would not leave Shirley alone; perhaps she might even go back to Eugene in time. There was maternal lamentation, but Shirley was buying no compromises.

That evening she also cut separation orders for Mr. Diego Romero, who took it very well for a young man who had been going steady with a beautiful girl for four years. "I want what's best for you, Shirley," he told her. "If finding God will make you happy, and it means our breaking up, well, that's it."

Shirley opened her Bible to II Corinthians 6 and read to him. "I'm sorry, Diego, I can't live any other way. I couldn't ever marry you unless I knew for sure that you belonged to God."

Diego put out his cigarette. "When does this guy Graham speak again?"

In the southwest corner of San Francisco, separated by the Junipero Serra Boulevard from the luxurious Park-merced residential community, lies the district known as Daly City. Here thousands of industrial workers, tradesmen, and machinists live in houses jammed together on twenty-five-foot lots. Inside one is always amazed at the pleasantness and tastefulness of the dwellings. It was in one of these homes that Eugene Plummer lived alone, until the day his daughter came back to fill his cup of happiness. For Shirley it was not a covenient location, but her mind was fixed. Once home, she called Pastor Petrie and told him she would be in church Sunday, and offered her shorthand and typing for any clerical work he might have. Then on a Tuesday evening she accepted a date from a new friend and arranged to go again to the Cow Palace.

Billy Graham spoke that night on temptation. He declared that the closer a man gets to Jesus Christ, the more he is exposed to the wiles, snares, and devices of Satan.

Shirley applied the message to her heart and was swept with remorse, for she had been so sure of her new righteousness. Hadn't she given up her mother and her boy friend because they were not Christians? Only a few hours ago it had seemed so clear that God had called her to place everything at the foot of the Cross, and she had responded. Now here was Billy Graham digging up unfinished business, showing her that there were a lot of other weak spots in her life.

Shirley had made her great decision because she wanted holiness; she wanted to be saved in perfection; she wanted to get away from sin completely. Yet when the evangelist had finished his message and was extending the invitation, her honest heart told her that the issue was not yet settled. She looked around; no one near her was moving. The voice of caution spoke; this was a new date—would anybody wait for her? Shirley shook her head. "I won't listen to it!" she decided, and stepping out of her seat, she walked down the ramp to the front of the platform.

Charles Riggs, head of the Billy Graham counseling program, is an ex-oil rigger from Pennsylvania with a keen eye for discerning out-of-the-ordinary situations. That evening he was in the counseling room when he noticed a girl weeping into her handkerchief, and being comforted by an older man wearing a counselor's badge. Tears are not unfamiliar to those in evangelistic work, but it is unusual for Graham Crusade inquirers to be counseled by a person of the opposite sex. Riggs walked up to them sympathetically.

"This is my daughter," explained Eugene Plummer, looking up. "She came forward tonight."

"Wonderful," said Charley. "Could you tell me about it?"

"I guess I was expecting too much," sobbed Shirley. "I

thought that if I obeyed God He would keep me from sin. I thought I could give up my cigarettes and my bad habits and just be perfect. I don't want to be half-saved. I don't want to have to be tempted all my life."

"It would be nice," agreed Charley, "but it doesn't happen to be the kind of world we live in. However, we are promised that if we confess our sins, God is faithful and just to forgive us and to cleanse us from all unrighteousness."

The old problem reared up again. "But I don't feel forgiven. How can I be forgiven for all I've done in just ten or fifteen minutes?"

Riggs shook his head. "It's not a matter of feeling at all, it's a matter of God's Word."

In the stock exhibit room of the Cow Palace that night for the first time Shirley Plummer found peace—not the peace of the saint but the peace of the forgiven sinner. She became a strong, witnessing Christian, and her church felt the power of God in her presence. As was expected, before long Diego came around and romance began to blossom again, until Shirley announced, "Diego, I've decided to fast until you become a Christian." Once he understood what she meant, Diego was shocked, bewildered, and finally he stormed protestingly out of the house. He hunted up Mavis and told her what was going on over in Daly City. "Your daughter is nuts in the head," he declared, "and furthermore, if she's going to disfigure herself by refusing to eat, I'm going to call the police."

Instead he went to the Cow Palace.

A century ago Shirley Plummer might have been a Carrie Nation or a Mary Slessor of Malabar, or perhaps a pioneer mother on the Oregon Trail. Three centuries ago she might have been a Susanna Wesley or an Anne Hutchinson, or one of the indomitable Quaker dames who threw early Boston into an uproar. Five centuries ago she might have been Joan of Arc. It is good to know God is forging such character in San Francisco.

Before the Crusade ended, strangely enough, both Mavis and Diego made decisions at the Cow Palace. Neither decision was completely fulfilled in life, yet there have been some changes. Diego is now a less possessive, more understanding lad. He appreciates better what happened to Shirley, and he realizes that unless her God becomes his God, his days with her are numbered.

In Mavis, too, a softening has taken place; she attends church with her husband and daughter, and her visits home are becoming friendlier and more frequent. She is less convinced that the answer to life is to be found in a bowling alley. As for Eugene, he is still not the easiest man in the world to live with; but the steps of a good man are ordered of the Lord, and as he and his daughter go out calling in new homes for their church each week, their hearts are quietly rejoicing in hope.

5. THE MAN WHO CAUGHT HIMSELF

"How did I keep checks floating? Well, I'd cash a hot check for, say, thirty dollars on a Saturday. Then on Monday I'd go someplace else and cash another check, and take the money down to the bank to cover the first one. Then three days later I'd write a larger check to cover the second one. Easiest thing in the world. Or if I was sure they didn't know me, I'd just make out a check to myself and sign it with anybody's name."

Arthur Richard Ramsden shook his head ruefully over his coffee. "Do you wonder I was nervous about talking to

Billy Graham? I'd done this sort of thing all over the country—in Indiana, Florida, Texas. Why, the FBI didn't even know about what went on in Dallas, because I lived there for two years under an assumed name. I had a conscience all right, but I figured if they ever caught up with me it would be ten years."

The life of Art Ramsden is a running commentary on the Biblical proverb, "The way of transgressors is hard." It is a kaleidoscope of jobs that didn't last, deals that failed, marriages that fell apart, hopes that faded in a blur of alcohol. He was a person who could do anything—shoe salesman, laundry operator, restaurant manager, chef—and he was clever enough to outwit anybody, until the day came when he outwitted himself.

At the age of five little Art sold newspapers on the street corners of Lexington, Kentucky, while his father peddled patent medicines through the hill country and his mother hired out as a housekeeper. There were nights when the grownups got absent-minded as to just who was taking care of Art and his older brother, Joel. Then the little newsboy would crawl into the bushes of someone's yard, or sleep away the warm summer nights on the town's sidewalks.

Three decades later the wheel came full circle, and Art Ramsden found himself on a May morning of 1958 in a broken-down car on the outskirts of San Jose, California. His liquor was gone, his money was gone, his second family had left him, he had nothing to eat and no place to stay, he was a fugitive from justice, and now his automobile had given out. He had spent the night stretched on the front seat, and as he rubbed the stiffness from his neck he wondered if ever again he would know the pleasure of a bath, a shave and a hot breakfast.

He knew that this was his day of decision. Snoring in the seat behind him was a hitchhiker with whom he had spent the last evening making plans for the robbery of a supermarket or a liquor store. In all his years of mixed-up living Art had never felt the need or the desire to resort to violence, but he had come to that place. He knew it was a point of no return, but when a man is desperate . . .

There was one other possibility. Somewhere in San Jose lived his brother.

The brothers mentioned in Biblical history did not, as a rule, illustrate the divine order of brotherhood. One reviews the lives of Cain and Abel, Jacob and Esau, Joseph and his brethren, Absalom and Amnon, James and John, the brethren of the Lord, and Jesus' story of the prodigal son, and wonders at the gap between the commandment "that he who loveth God love his brother also," and the actual performance. Probably the noblest example of brotherliness in kinship as recorded in Scripture, is the story of Andrew seeking out his brother Peter to bring him to Jesus (John 1:41-42).

The Rev. Joel Ramsden, now in his twentieth year in the ministry, is not as famous for his sermons as Billy Graham is, but he stands in the apostolic succession of St. Andrew, and he is a good brother. The years have not been easy for him since he left Trevecca College in Nashville to go into evangelistic work. When he came to California at forty years of age to organize a church, it meant starting at the beginning again. Yet the Lord has blessed Joel's life and his home, and he is not one to complain. Each evening as he laid his burdens at the Cross he would remember his brother Art, now unheard of since the Florida business. Each morning as he began his parish duties, he would first place his brother in the hands of the Lord.

It was a bit of a shock therefore to open the door one morning and find, instead of a tramp, his brother Art.

"Good heavens, Art, what's happened? Are you alone?"

"Yeah, I dropped a fellow off downtown. I—had a little car trouble."

"Ida," Joel called out, "come here, it's Art. He's back, praise the Lord. Come in here and get cleaned up, man. Had any breakfast?"

Afterward Joel listened to the whole story: about the phony checks written to meet payments on the house in Florida . . . the arrest in Jacksonville and the probation . . . the visit with mother and the hot check in Evansville that fell into the hands of the FBI . . . the second arrest and the "Dear John" from his wife, written to the jail . . . the release on bail pending trial . . . the divorce . . . the decision to jump his bond and begin a new life in Texas under the assumed name of Everett Nye . . . the second marriage in Dallas . . . the failures in restauranting and dry-cleaning and the new splurge of drinking and check-writing . . . the exit of Margie, who was now expecting but who had had enough . . . the flight from Dallas . . . and would Joel please tell him what to do now?

Joel Ramsden is a man with a strong, simple faith, and his knowledge of pastoral counseling has been gleaned mostly from life and from research in the pages of Holy Writ. His reply did not qualify him for a chair in the psychology of religion, neither did it measure as classic, but it rang true: "I think," he said, "that you should become a Christian, and then do what a Christian should do."

Joel then suggested that they might receive some guidance if they went together that night to the Cow Palace, where Billy Graham was conducting a Crusade. Art demurred: "I'm broke, I'm worried and nervous, and I've been drinking. Give me a couple of days first." He took Joel's offer of twenty dollars, found a room in a lodging house, and two nights later the family drove up to San Francisco and the Crusade.

Four times in the next ten days Art attended the meetings in the Cow Palace, and four times he watched hundreds of people go down the aisles at the invitation to accept Jesus Christ, but he never moved. He knew he had some accounts to straighten out with God that had been unbalanced since he left the little Sunday School back in Lexington. He knew that Billy was right when he said, "You are not here by accident"; knew that he ought to march up and make a decision—and yet what was there to gain compared with what there was to lose? He was still Everett Nye, wanted for forgery in Texas, and he still had not thrown over the idea of holding up a liquor store. It seemed such a simple answer to a host of problems.

He decided that he had better have one more talk with Joel before committing himself to anything. Joel arranged his calendar to suit, and for two hours one evening the matter was rehashed. Joel stuck to his counsel, until Art protested:

"It's easy for you to say, 'Leave it to the Lord'; you don't have facing you what I have."

"You become a Christian," replied Joel, "and the Lord will take care of you. He's promised to. Let's look again at that Thirty-seventh Psalm." There was more study, and then Joel closed his Bible. "Let's go talk to Billy Graham and see what he says," he suggested. "He's right over there in San Mateo."

"When?"

"Right now." Joel looked at his watch. "It's ten o'clock

—They ought to be back from the Cow Palace by the time we get there."

The night clerk at the Villa Motor Hotel was sorry that Dr. Graham could not be disturbed, but he had retired for the evening. Joel Ramsden was undismayed.

"What about Cliff Barrows? He ought to be just about back from his ten-thirty telecast unless I'm mistaken."

"Mr. Barrows? I'm not sure; I'll ring."

In thirteen years with Billy Graham, Cliff Barrows had never worked harder than he worked in the San Francisco Crusade. Telecasts local and national; weekly broadcasts of the "Hour of Decision"; special preaching assignments; leading the world's largest choir; singing duets with Bev Shea; monitoring the public address system in the Cow Palace; song-leading and introductions; coiling up the mike cord so it would not trip under Billy's feet as he preached; rehearsing, rehearsing, rehearsing . . . early morning until late at night . . . but Cliff Barrows came downstairs to the lobby to see two strange men.

Over and over the ground they went, three men in the quiet of the early morning hours, until at last Cliff spoke the word that struck home. "There's no escape from life," he said. "There's no escape—except to Christ." Slowly Art nodded his head, and Joel called for prayer. As the three men bowed, Arthur Richard Ramsden, alias Everett Nye, offered up his contrition to God and crossed the summit of the divide.

After the last "Amen" Barrows stood up. "What about it, Art?"

"I reckon I'm ready."

"Good. Let's go up to my room."

A telephone call was placed across the Bay to the home

of a friend of the Graham team and a prominent Christian layman, FBI agent Don Jones. Two hours later the fugitive was on his way to jail, but instead of fear he felt only relief that at last the long ordeal was over. What was sowed in Florida and Texas would be reaped in California.

Art ordered another cup of coffee and poured in plenty of sugar. "I never saw anything to beat the way the Lord took hold of my life after that," he ruminated. "I was out of that jail within a week and I haven't been back since, and with the help of God I don't intend to go back."

What happened, of course, was that brother Joel borrowed money on his automobile to raise the bail money. He then helped Art to find a job, and in a short time the latter was keeping himself busy thirteen hours a day, eight hours as a chef and five as a shoe salesman. The trial had yet to be faced, but meanwhile an odd circumstance helped to stave off Art's gravest problem. When he was released on bond from the San Francisco jail, he was presented with a warrant from Dallas County, Texas, arresting him on several counts of forgery. Instead of being charged as Everett Nye, however, his pseudonym was incorrectly spelled "Everett Tye," and Art received a few hours' grace until fresh papers could be flown up. That gave him time enough to telephone the sheriff of Dallas County and offer to pay off his obligations there at the rate of two hundred dollars per month. The sheriff accepted the offer and the heat was off.

During the week he spent in jail Art waived his right to a change of venue. To save expense to the federal government he agreed to be tried in California instead of Florida. When he appeared for his arraignment the district attorney told Federal Judge Charles Trevor, "This is the man, your Honor, whom you read about in the paper, and who gave himself up after attending the Billy Graham Crusade." A probation officer was then assigned to the case.

Art did one other thing while in jail—he wrote a letter to his wife Margie, asking forgiveness, begging for another chance, and inviting her to come to San Francisco. Margie was startled to find that her name had suddenly been changed from Nye to Ramsden, but the Associated Press story in the local paper verified her husband's letter, and west she came, bringing her baby daughter Stella.

"Yes," nodded Art Ramsden as he reached for the check, "Jesus Christ has been working one miracle after another in my life. Thirteen hours a day makes a good stint, but now I come home and sleep instead of going out drinking. This trailer court isn't too much, and the buggy has fallen apart again, and there's a probation officer looking over my shoulder, but the family's here—have you seen that baby?— and there's two hundred dollars going to Texas every month, and we're helping Joel get a new church started down in Santa Clara. By the way, did you happen to see last night's paper?"

He was standing at the cash register now, and from his wallet he drew out a fresh clipping which read:

> A 37-year-old itinerant cook who surrendered to FBI agents here last May after listening to evangelist Billy Graham speak, today was granted probation in U. S. District Court.
>
> Arthur Richard Ramsden of Redwood City told the federal agents following his surrender that he had jumped bail of $750 in Kissimmee, Fla., in September of 1956. He said he was facing charges there of passing worthless checks on an out-of-state bank.
>
> After he pleaded guilty to the interstate transportation

Hundreds respond to the call for decision at the conclusion of a Graham sermon in the Cow Palace.

Trained laymen explain the Scriptures and talk individually with those who crowd the counseling room.

Photos by Lonnie Wilson, Oakland Tribune

Faces in the crowd: old and young listen intently to Graham's words.

Pony-tailed teen-agers in Crusade choir listen to sermon.

The deaf receive the message through a Cow Palace interpreter.

Students pepper Graham with questions at San Francisco State College.

Willie Kirkland, San Francisco Giants' rookie right fielder, greets Graham at the Cow Palace on the night of his decision. (pp. 109-115)

of bogus checks, Federal Judge Charles Trevor gave Ramsden an eight-month suspended sentence, stating that he "wholeheartedly endorsed" the recommendation that Ramsden be placed on five years' probation.

Ramsden said after hearing Graham speak he decided to "straighten out my life." He said he had a drinking problem at the time he passed some $800 in worthless checks in Florida.

Today Judge Trevor asked him if he still drank and Ramsden said, "I am a Christian. I do not drink."

6. WILLIE KIRKLAND GETS A COACH

Willie Kirkland stood at the plate in Connie Mack Stadium, Philadelphia, swung the bat easily over his left shoulder and gazed at the right field wall, four hundred feet away. It was Sunday afternoon, June 22, 1958, and the Giants' rookie right-fielder faced a critical point in his career. Curiously enough, at the very moment Willie was tugging at his cap and tapping the rubber with the end of his bat, clear across the country in his home lot the crowds were beginning to gather in Seals Stadium to hear his friend Billy Graham at the final meeting of the San Francisco Bay Cities Crusade. But Kirkland's thoughts were understandably in Philadelphia, for it was the fourteenth inning and the score was tied.

Nearly seven weeks earlier the twenty-four-year-old rookie, playing his first season of National League baseball, had done something that superstitious sportsmen would never have approved and would only attribute to poor judgment. He had risen in his seat at an evangelistic meeting in the Cow Palace and, to use his own words, had walked forward to "give my life to Jesus Christ." The wise boys shook their heads when they saw his picture in the news. Mixing religion and baseball's not so good, they said; it's apt to upset your timing; and besides, saints aren't supposed to wear spikes, they're supposed to lie on them. The boy's in for trouble, they said.

Sure enough, in the days that followed Willie Kirkland's batting average curved gradually downward. He became worried, showed signs of pressing, and began swinging at bad balls. His teammates dug into him: "Have you seen the light yet, Willie? Better go to church and see if you can pick up some base hits." The fellows in the sports department at one of the metropolitan dailies dropped by the church editor's desk for a little kidding. "Have you noticed what's happened to your boy Willie? Looks like Graham didn't take—better change his religion." Finally manager Bill Rigney pulled Kirkland from the outfield and sent him packing to the minor leagues in disgrace; there was no room on the Giants for a .167 hitter.

For three weeks Willie played with the Phoenix team of the Pacific Coast League and practiced hitting within the "strike zone." His slump continued; but unexpectedly he was recalled to the Giant lineup for the road trip, and now he was being given his first new chance against the Phillies.

For thirteen innings he had gone hitless while the Phillies' Ray Semproch and the Giants' Johnny Antonelli had staged a superb pitchers' duel. The score was 4 to 4, and nobody had hit on either side for three innings. What could Kirkland do? Theoretically he was the man to break up the game; he had done it just four weeks before in this same stadium, poking up one of those four-hundred-footers in the ninth inning. It was his last solid hit before being farmed out to Phoenix.

Now Semproch was winding up for the pitch, and Willie

Kirkland breathed a prayer. He did not normally pray in the batter's box, but the time called for unusual measures. "Lord," he said quietly, "if you're ever going to let me hit a ball, let me hit it now." It was a fast pitch, high, and Willie leaned his 195-pound, six-foot frame into it. There was a crack; the ball sailed on a low trajectory up, up, and over the wall in right field. Next morning Bob Stevens reported in the San Francisco *Chronicle*:

> Walloping Willie Kirkland, complete with toothpick and muscles, returned to the Giant batting order today after a short career in Phoenix to rip a 14th-inning home run and give the San Francisco club a dramatic 5 to 4 victory. . . .

Willie Kirkland was only one of three members of the San Francisco Giants who found new purpose and direction in life at the Billy Graham Crusade. The others were pitcher Al (Red) Worthington and outfielder Bob Speake, both of whom became within a few weeks dynamic, witnessing Christians. Willie still has trouble expressing himself; he has yet to master the art of public speaking. Since finishing high school in Detroit he has spent most of his time studying baseball. Of the millions of American boys who play ball, he was one of the rare ones who showed the raw potential of some day moving up to big time. Because he was easygoing, likable and friendly, he found plenty of people willing to help him as he made the slow progression from amateur to semi-pro to Class D to Class B to Class A and Triple-A. In the summer of 1956 an old-timer, Bill Taylor, spent day after day improving Willie's weak side—his fielding—by hitting him ground balls and fly balls in monotonous succession. "Like to run me to death," said Willie.

Yet no one in those years spoke to the young rookie about what lay beyond the world of baseball, beyond all sports and actions of this life. At the age of fifteen he had gone forward to be baptized one Sunday in the Corinthian Baptist Church of Detroit, but it is not easy for a ball player to attend services; when Christians are in church, the rest of America is often in the ball park. As he traveled from one league to another, from Maryville, Tennessee, to Danville, Virginia, to St. Cloud, Minnesota, to Sioux City, Iowa, to the Escojido team in Ciudad Trujillo, Dominican Republic, and finally to Minneapolis, Willie Kirkland learned a lot about life but not much about God.

Then came the big chance with the Giants, the sensational showing at spring training, and the move to San Francisco. One Sunday evening Willie was invited by a friend to attend the services at the Third Baptist Church, the largest Negro church in the city. The pastor, Dr. F. D. Haynes, was a member of the executive committee of the Billy Graham Crusade which was just commencing. The evening speaker was the Rev. Howard Jones, a Cleveland pastor who had recently returned from conducting some unusual evangelistic meetings in Ghana and Liberia, and who was now serving as an associate evangelist with Billy Graham. Kirkland was introduced to Mr. Jones, and the minister invited him to the Cow Palace. On the following evening the Giants' right-fielder was taken to a little room marked "Private" and, while the flashbulbs popped, he shook hands with Graham. Then he went to a box seat and listened to the sermon.

There are no new sins today [Billy was saying], just new sinners; no new crimes, just new criminals; no new evil, only evil doers; no new pleasure, only pleasure seekers. The devil has invented no new gimmicks. Sin and its accompanying effects are and always have been the same. There is, however, a new word that has become popular— escapism. Men for centuries have been trying to escape the realities of life and to shirk their responsibilities to God. It is one of the tricks of Satan. One of the great designs and plans of Satan for you is that you may find a measure of temporary satisfaction in the escapism he offers.

Thousands of people are caught in the clutches of escapism. Instead of facing up to the realities of sin and defeat in your life, you're trying to hide in an illusive and imaginary world. The Bible says there is no possible way of escape, not even through suicide. Sooner or later we must leave our dream world and face up to the facts of God, sin and judgment.

A thousand and one psychological problems have gripped millions because of sin. Personalities are warped by frustration, fear and nervous tension. Thousands read cheap novels and get vicarious, imaginative thrills out of the experiences of others. There is the flight into passion, appetite and desire. Poor, frustrated, deluded souls run like frightened beasts into the jungle of worldly pleasures only to emerge more miserable than ever before.

The Bible teaches that with Christ in your life, you can face the realities of life even though they are harsh. The Grace of God will give you greater joy and pleasure than any dream into which you may try to escape. We want genuine joy and happiness, but it is not something artificially stimulated by sinful pleasure. It is a joy that comes through trusting Christ.[1]

When the invitation was given that night, Willie Kirkland was one of the first to walk down and take his stand in front of the rostrum. "Rich or poor, young or old, white

[1] Reported in Oakland *Tribune*, May 1, 1958.

or colored, you come," Billy said, and Kirkland came, to be joined by a blond, husky young man with a crew-cut and a Bible in his hand. In the counseling room the ballplayer was recognized and the grapevine passed the word, so that when he emerged with his Gospel of John in hand, the newsmen were waiting for him. Willie grinned as he faced them and admitted that he had made a decision for Christ. It was a natural headline, the break for which the press had been waiting: MAJOR LEAGUE STAR CONVERTED AT COW PALACE. The reporters rushed to their phones.

When the news was brought to Billy Graham he reacted swiftly. "This boy must be protected!" The press was called and the story was graciously toned down to the extent that Willie Kirkland was taken out of the spotlight and mentioned simply as one of the 11,000 who attended the service. This co-operation on the part of the newspapers is an indication of the rapport that existed with Billy Graham, for the pressure on a new Christian in the right field at Seals Stadium could have been unbearable.

What really happened to Willie that night at the Cow Palace? It was a restoration to what had been taught him by his mother in the early days in Birmingham, Alabama, and to what he had been baptized into at the Corinthian Baptist Church of Detroit. The words that Graham spoke seemed to carry for him the ring of authority and truth. "Everything that man said was right, at least it seemed right to me," reflected the young outfielder. "I felt as if God were saying to me, 'Willie, I forgive you for everything,' and there came a peace into my heart."

The going was not easy after that, for competition is fierce on the San Francisco Giants, and Willie felt the testing of the Lord. After the three weeks in Phoenix his average headed back toward .300, and his long ball was again breaking up major league ball games, but he was far from satisfied.

One of Kirkland's fellow Christians on the Giants' team, pitcher Al Worthington, has developed a kind of baseball theology. "Playing ball in the minors," says Al, "is like sitting in a church all your life and never getting to Christ." His words are reminiscent of St. Paul: "Know ye not that they which run in a race run all, but one receiveth the prize? So run, that ye may obtain" (I Cor. 9:24). For Worthington, for Bob Speake and for Kirkland, there may be few years in the big leagues and there may be many, but they have the assurance that in some mysterious way, they are signed up for life in the Great Ball Club in the Sky.

7. THE LORD AND THE COUNT

Count Maximilian von Styria has been described in many ways by his admirers, but no one has ever thought of calling him a churchman. It is as hard to picture him an ordained, practicing deacon or elder as it is to picture the continental aristocracy suddenly gone middle class. Even since the Billy Graham Crusade, when the Count surprised everyone by making a decision for Jesus Christ, there has been no gravitation toward any particular church. His friends are praying for him; for the present it had better be left at that. Not that von Styria is outside the Church; far from it. He happens to be outside the communicant membership of any local church, but in which church would he feel at home? It is not easy to be the last of the ruling house of Styria. A Bible class in the drawing room of the chateau of the Countess de Lyons—this would be delightful. Or an evening at the Cow Palace, listening to Billy Graham . . .

Seven hundred years ago the king of Bohemia elevated

the house of Styria to the nobility. Over the years the family played its role in the history of Central Europe, meanwhile acquiring vast estates: flour mills in Hungary, castles and cattle in Austria, horses and stables in what is now Czechoslovakia. Who would not wish to be born under such a crest? Young Maximilian grew up in Vienna in the gay days of schmaltz and waltz before 1914. At the court of the Hapsburgs he moved easily and familiarly, and attended courses at the University of Vienna. After the war he spent some time in art academies in Paris, and then took a diploma in engineering from the University of Heidelberg.

The period between the two world wars saw the collapse of many noble estates, von Styria's among them. One government after another nibbled at the family properties until everything was confiscated which had not been prudently deposited abroad. That meant travel, and so the family traveled—to America, to Sweden, to England, always first class, always among the aristocrats and those of noble lineage.

Maximilian liked America when he first came here at age eleven, and his impressions deepened in later visits. When the time came—as it came to many a nobleman—for him to start earning a living, his imagination went stateside. America was free and big. Here he could launch a business without upsetting the protocol of the years and without disturbing every commercial house in Europe. Here he could open a designing studio for manufactured products, and he did in New York City. Distinguished customers came to his door, including one of America's leading can companies. After he moved his studio to Los Angeles the firm invited him to come to its San Francisco offices and be its chief designer.

Ultramontane bishops were almost daily visitors at the house of Styria in Maximilian's early days, but after his sister married a Lutheran noble the whole family followed her into the Lutheran Church. Important as the change was, it did not basically alter the faith of the young boy in Jesus Christ. His trust in the Savior was established early and remained throughout his life, as he sought in the ways of largesse open to the nobility to express the love of Christ for his fellow man.

To be sure the Count was no political reformer; he took up no cudgels for the downtrodden masses. Neither did he venture far out of his familiar fields into philosophical or theological pursuits. He was a man of his times, an engineering designer, and a kindly Christian gentleman. He was also an artist whose paintings sought to capture the glory of Christ in the handiwork of nature.

Count Maximilian's new relationship with his Lord began with a tremendous birthday party for the Countess de Lyons at her ninety-two-room chateau in Hillsborough. The Countess was asked by Christian friends to make it an opportunity to introduce Billy Graham to some of the older families of the peninsula, and being a Graham admirer herself, she was delighted to do so. It proved to be a pleasant evening, and Billy came down after he had finished at the Cow Palace. He was presented to some four hundred guests in the great ballroom, made some remarks and won some friends, including Maximilian. The Count had never heard or seen Dr. Graham before, and for a good reason. His social calendar being what it is, he has little use for a radio or a television set. One of Dr. Graham's secretaries, Miss Christine Jarrett, engaged the Count in conversation. Would he like to visit the Cow Palace? She offered him her pass and introduced him to other members of the team:

Mrs. Leighton Ford, sister of Dr. Graham; two English girls, Miss Beryl Gilbertson and Miss Patricia Campion, and others.

Once Count Maximilian began attending the Crusade meetings his social calendar went into eclipse. He found the Cow Palace irresistible. He enjoyed the tremendous music of the choir, the new friends, the happy spirit of the occasions. Especially he loved the evangelist's sermons. The Count had never heard preaching like this, never heard the Bible made so interesting, never felt the power of the Gospel to be so gripping. Once many years before he had heard a somewhat similar message at a great meeting; it was when he was working in Los Angeles and was commissioned to illustrate a magazine edited by Mrs. Aimée Semple MacPherson. When he came to Angelus Temple Aimée would pause in her sermon, point to the distinguished European nobleman in the midst, and give glory to God. Maximilian did not attend very often. He recognized that Billy's was a message of the same sort, yet there were differences, too.

One night Billy preached a sermon on the subject of Naaman the Syrian, who was cured of leprosy by obeying Elisha's command to wash in the river Jordan (II Kings 5). "You have a moral disease that the Bible illustrates by leprosy," declared the evangelist. "This disease is slow, sure, deliberate and deadly. In the end it will get you. Yet Jesus Christ can heal you as he healed Naaman the general. He can make you every whit whole."

As the invitation was given that evening, some of the ladies sitting in the box prepared to move toward the front, where they would take their places as counselors. Count Maximilian rose politely and smiled. "I'm going with you." They looked at him, surprised, wondering

whether to smile back, hardly believing their ears. The
word was carried quickly to those in charge of follow-up,
and an old friend came over to counsel with the new inquirer.

Exactly what happened to this man at the Billy Graham
Crusade? As far as his relationship to the ecclesiastical life
of the community is concerned, he is still good friends with
several peninsula ministers and has chosen to sit under no
one of them. Jesus Christ has made His most noticeable
impact on the Count's personal life. He no longer considers
his life or his possessions to be his own; they belong to God.
He treats the Lord as his best Friend, and talks to Him
familiarly, preferring to make his own prayers. He has
bought a Revised Standard Version of the Bible and is reading it. He has sensed the guidance of the Holy Spirit in
matters of daily living.

Such piety was perhaps not too uncommon a century ago,
when gentility was in flower, but it was rare enough in
San Francisco 1958. The Count, although he brought
friends and groups to the Cow Palace in his car night after
night, has not the gifts of an evangelist. He senses keenly
how ineffective the Crusade was in reaching the stratum
of the city that he knows so well: the world of the opera,
the concert and the soirée. San Francisco likes its parties
and does not care to give them up for Billy Graham or anyone else. Maximilian's friends are charmed to find that the
Count is now in communication with Jesus Christ—
charmed, but not convinced. The Count on the other hand
has made an intriguing discovery: that being around Christian people can be an exciting and an entertaining experience.

Here is a seed sown by the Crusade that landed outside the conventional orbit of evangelical church life, in an area uncultivated during San Francisco's hundred years of history. In biology such a variation is called a "sport," and is not considered too significant. The New Testament teaches, however, that when a seed is encouraged with good soil and water it can produce an amazing amount of fruit. Or, as a member of the team, the Rev. Joseph Blinco, once expressed it to the ministers of the Bay Area, God has a most disconcerting habit of laying His hands on the wrong man.

8. THE PROFESSION THAT BECAME A VOCATION

Sergeant Bob Lutz, combat instructor, U. S. Marine Corps, shook his head as he closed his wallet and slipped it back into his pocket. She was a beautiful girl, no doubt about it, but whatever had come over her? He decided he had a lot to learn about women; and the great trouble was, Valerie was the woman for him. He picked up the pen and checked his wrist watch. The ETD was just two hours away, but he was in battle dress and ready. The orders were cut twenty-four hours earlier, when he was first alerted for overseas shipment. The line marked "destination" was left blank, but any newspaper headline could have supplied the information: Sergeant Lutz was about to be flown to the beaches of Lebanon. Meanwhile he was thinking about the one personal item that was buried deep in his duffle bag—an engagement ring.

"Hi, Val," he wrote, "I can't really say much of anything, just good-bye . . ."

So ended a strange love story in which the key earthly

role was played by an evangelist who never heard of either Valerie or Bob. But this is not Billy Graham's story, nor is it the sergeant's, for that matter. It is the story of a student nurse whose profession was transformed into a vocation.

Deft was the word for Valerie. Once she spotted her goal, she moved swiftly to attain it, and so sure was she of herself that it seemed nothing in heaven or earth could stand in her way. Behind that demure face and attractive figure was the purposefulness of a steam roller. As a student at a popular high school on the eastern shore of San Francisco Bay, she had not taken long to spy out Mr. Robert Lutz. How natural that they should begin dating, and then going together! People commented on how nicely they seemed to be matched, he a basketball star, she a sorority member—the aristocracy of the campus.

Valerie Robertson had other plans, too. She was a good student, and had been serving as a nurse's aide in a local hospital. She was not sure exactly why nursing interested her, but her girl friend was going into training, and there was a prospect of excitement. Hadn't Florence Nightingale's life been filled with adventure? Valerie was willing to be a Nightingale or a Jane Addams, if it came to that. She applied for a scholarship which was granted annually by a local medical association, and was awarded it in her senior year, shortly before graduation. About the time that Bob was reporting to boot camp, Valerie enrolled in the Kaiser Foundation School of Nursing in Oakland.

A year later Corporal Lutz flew back to the Bay Area from a tour of duty on Okinawa, and the young lovers took their holiday together. A ring blossomed on the hand of the student nurse. Word had been passed down that Bob was about to be tagged for a special training school in Washington, and the outlook was bright. Val had her career and she had her man. Then came the winter, and the student nurses were transferred to Palo Alto for three months' special training with mental patients at the Veterans' Administration hospital.

Now Valerie's life began to be filled with disturbed and disturbing people. What do you do, for example, with a man who looks you in the eye and tells you that he is Jesus Christ? "You dance with him," said the nurse supervisor. But what do you say to him? What happens to the nurse's cool efficiency now? Valerie suddenly felt very young, very insecure. For the first time in her life she was faced daily with problems that were beyond her. As she worked with these victims of fear and rejection she discovered how really helpless she was, and she turned instinctively to her fellow student nurses for support.

One girl in particular, Irene, attracted Valerie's attention. She was certainly a charming person, but she had an extra quality that Valerie could not quite fathom. She seemed to have a beautiful soul. She never seemed to join in petty criticism; she had a good word for everyone, and there was a calmness about her that set Valerie to wondering. Then a friend confided the secret: Irene was a Christian.

Well, who wasn't? Hadn't Valerie gone to church all her life? And Bob too for that matter; but it had become boring and they had stopped attending some time ago. As she became better friends with Irene, Valerie was told that several of the nurses were Christians, and that some of them were planning to attend a counseling class on their evening off. It seemed that Billy Graham was coming to the Cow Palace. Would Val like to take in the class with her friends?

A few nights later Irene spoke again to her new friend. Some of the girls were going to gather in one of their rooms for prayer, and Valerie might like to attend. Thus far Val had managed her life very nicely without prayer. She had been in prayer groups, of course, and had invariably felt embarrassed. It struck her that it was always the queer ones who seemed to do most of the praying. That night, however, Valerie prayed a spoken prayer for the first time, and it reflected the situation in which she found herself. She asked for guidance in helping and understanding her patients.

Meanwhile Billy Graham had arrived and the meetings had begun. Irene and Valerie and their friends formed a carload, and on the second night they drove to the Cow Palace. Valerie's attitude was mildly patronizing throughout the early part of the service, but when the sermon began, and the strong, simple phrases came forth, she realized what it was that Irene had and she did not have. She saw how casually she had shut God out of every part of her life. Jesus Christ had been discarded for years as either a minor prophet or a myth. As the message drew to a close, and she sensed that she would be invited to "go forward," her heart began the telltale quickening.

At last he finished speaking, and the people were moving out of their seats here and there. Valerie took a deep breath, and Billy began to speak again. "Christ could have healed the man with the withered arm," he said, "but he wanted the man to do something, as an act of faith, so he first told him to stretch his arm forth. I am asking you to stretch forth your life as an act of faith, and come and give yourself to Jesus Christ."

Valerie looked at the aisle to her right. There were so

many to crawl over before she could reach it! She stood up . . .

The Christian life, Billy Graham had said, would bring peace; but there was another phrase he used—something about problems increasing. It seemed to Valerie that now a conflict more serious than any she had ever known was raging in her breast. If she were to put Christ first, then Val would have to take second place. The steam roller would have to go. Those deft tricks by which she imposed her will on other people, and got what she wanted—what about them? What about Bob? Did she really love him, or was this just more of the same?

"Put God first . . . put God first . . . put God first." Valerie began to examine all her motivations, and the battlefield spread. Her mind was in a turmoil as she went about her daily tasks. She began to see her patients in a new light—not just as cases, but as people. And after a fortnight of indecision, she gave the ring back to Bob. She had not been wearing it, she told him. She was confused, and wanted time to pray about the whole thing; right now they seemed to have different interests and goals.

"What's the pitch?" he insisted.

"I don't know," she confessed. "It's hard to explain, except that at the Cow Palace that night I realized that I'd never allowed myself to be completely humble, so I said, 'Christ, here I am, do what you want with me.'"

Once the break was made, the tension seemed to lift, and Valerie began to give evidence of being a changed person. Her attitude toward her work was affected by her prayer life, and her relationships with her sister nurses were altered by her testimony. No longer did she insist on imposing her will on people. There was a new receptivity, an openness of heart and mind that was readily apparent, especially to the patients. She began praying for them, and was soon having success with patients that none of the staff had been able to reach.

Valerie joined with Irene and the others to bring groups of nurses to the Cow Palace. She began attending church, and when asked to speak it was with a new kind of poise and a new kind of assurance that she testified, for it was evident that she had made a pilgrimage to the Cross. In time she was transferred to other healing centers for further training, and a unique kind of activity seemed to surround her wherever she went. Instead of being a student nurse looking for excitement, Valerie manifested a new purpose in her work. She moved among her patients—the paraplegics and quadruplegics, the victims of multiple sclerosis, muscular distrophy, cerebral vascular accidents, polio—in a spirit of prayer and encouragement. She continued to pray with other students and with patients; and when Billy Graham came to Los Angeles, where she was serving, they arranged for a carload of patients to attend.

Occasionally Valerie went on a date, and when she did, the young man was in for a surprise. One such person turned out to be an ex-Bible school student who had followed the example of Demas (II Tim. 4:10) and had forsaken Christ for worldly ways. In a mysterious way the Lord prevailed upon him to reconsider after five years, and to apply for readmission.

But what of Bob? Valerie still thinks of him, and they still write, but if it is God's will that they should be brought together again, He has not yet made it clear. Bob's life has not been untouched; he too made his decision at the Cow Palace, but the role of a Christian marine is not easy, and world events have kept Bob's spiritual growth more or less in suspended animation. Someday, perhaps, their paths will cross once more, and Valerie will be able to share with Bob what Christ has done for her.

Until then. . . . .

9. THE BULLET THAT GOD DEFLECTED

George Matthews lurched into his apartment and threw his overcoat on the bed. The evening had cost him over a hundred dollars and it left him in a bad mood. He walked over and stared at a full front page of the San Francisco *Examiner*, Scotch-taped to the wall. It showed a strapping patrolman, hair iron-gray at the temples and handsome features resembling his own, carrying a hysterical woman off the Bay bridge over his shoulder.

COP RESCUES WOULD-BE SUICIDE

read the caption. The date on the newspaper was November, 1957, just two months ago.

George spat at the picture and turned to his bed table. There was something that interested him—a gleaming .38 service revolver, the only thing left to remind him of eight years in the California State Highway Patrol. All the rest —holster, belt, handcuffs, breeches, boots, jacket, cap—he had given away. "You can resign," the captain had said, "or we will press charges. Take your choice." Matthews picked it up and held it lovingly in his hand. "Is this the day?" he asked in a low mutter. He had his plans made. He would take a room in a motel on MacArthur Boulevard, call the Oakland Police Department, inform them of his address and intention, and then blow his brains out. Nothing messy. No hunting for a body. Just—exit. "I am poured out like water

. . . and thou hast brought me into the dust of death" (Ps. 22:14-15).

No, he decided, this wasn't the day. He still had a few bucks left—mighty few. In two months he had gone through nearly the entire four thousand dollars retirement pay he had built up in the Patrol. It had been some blowout. Palm Springs . . . New York . . . the Copacabana . . . the Stork Club . . . *My Fair Lady*. He took out his wallet and laid it beside the gun. One more martini, and then to bed. Nothing like a martini—and nobody mixed them like old George.

The following evening George felt better. He had slept, eaten, and was ready for another bout with the gang he knew would be gathered at the bar on Oakland's College Avenue. Where would the party be tonight? It didn't matter. What did matter was livin' it up—before oblivion.

On the way to the bar he strolled past the open door of a church. Inside he could hear the choir singing a familiar number. Nostalgia of youth, he thought; Sunday School and all that. He stopped and listened. Then for some unexplained reason he walked in. "For a day in thy courts is better than a thousand" (Ps. 84:10).

Today George Matthews has an insatiable hunger for Jesus Christ. He has lost his wife, his friends, his job, and all his money. He has given up his apartment and has moved into a rooming house owned by a church member. His rent is not paid and he needs a haircut. He is dependent upon the kindness of churchfolk until his manliness cries out in protest. Because he is a Christian and no longer the congenital liar that he was, he applies for a job and tells the truth. People are sorry, but they cannot afford the risk.

George, caught in the midst of adversity, is spending much time in the Book of Psalms: "All thy waves and thy billows are gone over me" (Ps. 42:7). God is testing His servant.

The story of George Matthews began thirty-eight years ago on San Francisco's College Hill, where he was born into a fine Christian home. His father was a janitor. When World War II broke out George joined the Coast Guard and became boatswain's mate aboard a destroyer escort. During the four and one-half years he spent in the Pacific George "grew up." He decided that God was a grand and beautiful fable; that Christians were an odd-ball group he did not wish to associate with because they never seemed to have any fun.

In 1944 George had a narrow escape from death. He was stationed aboard a fire barge moored between two munitions ships at Port Chicago in upper San Francisco Bay. Having an unexpected couple of hours' leave, he wandered down to the village. Just as he reached the edge of town the ships exploded, he was knocked over, and the barge crew and three hundred stevedores were killed. As he reflected on it he made no theological deductions whatever. Some people, he decided, were lucky and others weren't. That's it.

Within a few weeks he was married to Marie, a girl he had gone with during school days at Mission High. For a few years after his discharge they lived in San Francisco, he a bank teller and she a telephone operator. In 1947 he took the examination for the Highway Patrol, and two years later he was accepted, given a motorcycle and put to work.

It is a well-known fact that the uniform changes the man. George the bank teller was just another man on the street, but George the state trooper was a different matter. When he swaggered into a bar with his gun in its holster all eyes turned in his direction. Until now women had not paid him extraordinary attention, but suddenly he was meeting more and more of them. Most of the fellows in the Patrol were men of integrity, family men, but a few of them traded on their occupations, and George chose the fast pack. "Get a date," they would say, "and come on over; we're having a little get-together."

In 1956 Marie moved out for good.

On the job George was a good patrolman and won several special commendations for his work. Off the job he found it impossible to stop the merry-go-round. One day a telephone call came to the captain of the Patrol: "I think you should do something about one of your officers who has been spending a lot of time at my daughter's. She no longer has a husband, and there's no reason why Mr. Matthews shouldn't marry her."

The captain was puzzled. "Madam, Mr. Matthews is already married . . ."

The speaker that evening in the church on College Avenue was the Rev. Roy Hession, an evangelist from Great Britain. His subject was, "I am the Door." George sat as if rooted to the spot: "my heart and my flesh crieth out for the living God" (Ps. 84:2). The offering plate was passed and he placed on it the money he had intended to spend in the bar. After that he began attending church on Sunday mornings, and his drinking sessions were less extreme, partly because he had now run through all his money. The revolver stayed by the bedside. George read the Gospel of John and the book Mr. Hession had written, *Calvary Road*. He decided that he could accept Jesus Christ intellectually, as he would accept the existence of Julius Caesar or Napoleon.

The church was beginning to make preparations for the coming of Billy Graham to the Cow Palace, and George was asked if he would be willing to serve as an usher. He agreed, though with some wariness. He was far from being an "insider"; he had never prayed, his drinking pattern was still in the picture, he had not joined the church, and he felt beyond the pale of any Gospel of salvation through Jesus Christ.

The first Sunday at the Cow Palace was a most impressive experience; Billy Graham was a great preacher, there was no doubt of it. For George, however, it was someone else's show. He told himself that he was giving way to no emotions or spells. In spite of his resistance the meetings at the Cow Palace continued to attract him even on nights when he was not scheduled to usher. He wondered if after all he was not one of those whose hearts were slowly being hardened toward God.

On Saturday night, May 10, Billy preached over a nation-wide telecast from the Cow Palace on the subject, "The Wickedest Man Who Ever Lived." It was the story of Manasseh, king of Judah, which is told in II Kings 21 and II Chronicles 33. Manasseh departed from the faith of his fathers, engaged in sorcery and idolatry, and encouraged human sacrifice even with his own children. He was taken captive into Babylon, but after he humbled himself before the God of his fathers he was restored to his throne in Jerusalem.

"Oh, the love of God," cried Billy. "Oh, the Mercy of God! This man, who had committed unthinkable crimes, was not only pardoned, he was restored to his kingdom. Neither you nor I would have done it, but God did."

Restored? George Matthews started. Was it possible that there was hope for him? He had been wicked, but not as

wicked as Manasseh. He hardly dared hold the thought—
was it possible that he could be restored to the Highway
Patrol? That he could become a Christian police officer?
Was it possible that God would forgive his sins? That night
George made his commitment. The Holy Spirit drew him
from his seat and Jesus Christ was received by faith. No
longer was it merely the intellectual acceptance; now the
heart too said "Yes!" George felt as did Christian in *A Pil-
grim's Progress* that a great load had rolled from his shoulders at the foot of the Cross.

The next day the gun was sold for fifteen dollars. The
money was given to the "Operation Andrew" program of
his church so that others could ride the bus to the Cow
Palace.

Night after night he went back. Billy spoke forty-five
times in the great arena, and George was there forty of
them. But what a difference when the invitation was given!
No wringing of hands now, no hesitations, no fears, simply
joy as he bowed his head with the others. He bought a
Bible. He obtained temporary work. He looked up his es-
tranged wife and brought her to the meetings, but she was
seeking help in another direction, and had no desire for a
renewal of her marriage. He looked up his old friends but
they avoided him. "The word is out on you," they told
him. "All you will do is invite us to the Crusade. But if you
will give up this Christian 'kick' we'll get you a job mixing
drinks in Las Vegas."

There came a day when the meetings ended, and George
Matthews was no longer needed as an usher. The crowds,
the excitement were gone; all that was left was a church
around the corner and a clean, plain upstairs room. A *Head
of Christ* by Sallman hangs on the wall, as George sits reading his Bible. Now the road is hard and steep, and where

it leads no one knows, but this much is sure: where George goes, he does not walk alone. "I had rather be a doorkeeper in the house of my God, than to dwell in the tents of wickedness" (Ps. 84:10).

10. DR. WARRINGTON COMES BACK

Dr. Bruce Warrington sat writing at the desk in the office of his dental clinic. The neat, subdued atmosphere of the room indicated much about the man. Outside the window were the leafy shade trees of a prosperous peninsula city, while across the hall was some of the expensive equipment that provides the working tools of the oral surgeon. He was making a copy of some rough notes.

> This is a freely given and honest account of my experience in making a decision for Christ at the Billy Graham San Francisco Crusade.

His pen hesitated a moment, then resumed writing rapidly.

> At the time the Crusade opened in San Francisco I was living alone, a depressed, lonesome, heartsick person. I had recently separated from my wife and two sons after years of misunderstanding, petty arguments, quarrels, and a complete breakdown of communications within our home. To fill the lonely hours I was drinking heavily. I was unable to sleep for any period and was relying on sedatives for sufficient rest. My mental health was at a low ebb and my physical health was beginning to show signs of a breakdown.
> Lest this be misunderstood, let me say that great effort had been made to resolve our family problems. We had

tried psychological counseling, psychiatry and human relations studies, and to no avail—our problems got progressively worse.

Two things Bruce Warrington never expected to be: either a dentist or a Christian. When he graduated from the University of California's school of zoology he hoped to get into medical school. The depression, however, disrupted a good many plans; and after marriage, he engaged in factory personnel work until the outbreak of World War II. When in 1943 the Army took over the U. C. Medical and Dental Schools, Bruce was turned down by the one and accepted by the other. Under the speed-up he graduated in 1946 and, at thirty-three years of age, moved to the peninsula with his wife and two little sons, and established a practice.

The emotional disturbances that plagued the Warringtons' lives appeared early in marriage, but became acute after they moved. Week-end drinking parties became the scenes of unlovely arguments. Fern Warrington had a habit of being late to everything. They could not agree on the children's discipline. If it were a trip or a vacation, there was sure to be a quarrel over it.

When the Korean War broke out Lieutenant Warrington was called up, commissioned and ordered to camp. It did not take Bruce and Fern long to find the bar at the Officers' Club. There were more scenes and public embarrassments. Family life disintegrated to the point where Bruce in desperation and disgust applied for overseas duty.

For sixteen months he was attached to the mobile army surgical hospital immediately behind the front lines in Korea, while the family returned home. He came back from the wars to find that Fern had been taking treatment from a psychologist who had helped her to stop drinking. In the joy of reunion there was temporary peace, but Bruce soon discovered to his dismay that everything was now being interpreted psychologically. A fresh crop of disagreements began to sprout, and it was evident on all sides that there was still no working relationship, no understanding, no real love being shown.

Bruce began to cast about for help. He engaged a psychiatrist for several months at twenty-five dollars an hour. The psychiatrist had plenty of sympathy for his professional colleague, but that was not enough. Bruce tried living alone in a motel. He and Fern took a course in human relations from a nearby institute, and learned public speaking and the cultivation of a "positive" frame of mind. Then one day he discovered bank-account trouble and considered it the last straw. For the third time he moved out in a rage and took an apartment downtown. "This time," he told Fern, "it's divorce, and I'm going to get it." He began drinking in earnest . . .

He continued to write on the plain white paper:

> It was at this time that I was influenced to attend the Crusade by a wonderful Christian who realized its potential value to me. I had not been a church member in the twenty-five years of my adult life and had rarely been in a church during this time. I wasn't opposed to religion. I simply had no faith in it for myself.

The nurses at the clinic were concerned at what they saw happening to their boss, but what could they do? Personal matters are not professional matters. One of them, Diane, had put Dr. Warrington's name on the prayer list at her church, and realized that she now must wait for God's opportunity.

It came during a lighthearted coffee break at the clinic, when a visiting oral surgeon had finished a comical story of his early Sunday School days.

"Let's sing a hymn," suggested Bruce owlishly.

"I can, you know," laughed Diane, "I'm practicing for the Billy Graham choir that's going to sing at the Cow Palace."

"No!"

"Well, what did Billy say about sin last night?" The topic had become an amiable one in clinic conversation. Diane took full advantage of it. "He said that God's love is so amazing that He erases our sins from His mind as a tape recorder erases its sound track."

"He did, eh?" It happened that the doctor's hands were particularly unsteady that morning. As a patient left he remarked, "I'm having a rough day. I think I'll go up and sing with you tonight."

"Love to have you come," said Diane, controlling her feelings. "Blanche and I are driving up and you can ride with us."

The first night I attended I was most impressed by the entire service, but was not moved personally. I was deeply puzzled by the large number of people who responded to the invitation to accept Christ. I felt the power of the response without understanding what was happening, but I felt I had to return.

Diane was upset. Billy Graham had chosen for his subject that night "sex," and she felt he couldn't have missed the target more completely. "Why in heaven's name couldn't he have talked about something else?" she scribbled to

Blanche. "I guess he didn't know what a time we had getting the boss here."

> I attended frequently after that, and each successive time the basic truths of Mr. Graham's messages became more real and more compelling, and I began to feel I was getting close to what had been missing in my life these many years.

The significant discovery of Dr. Warrington during his nights at the Cow Palace was that even before he could seek a solution to his problems, he needed to find an inner peace and joy. He was aware that he had tried just about everything except Jesus Christ. The messages he was hearing emphasized the Cross, where an atonement was made for the sins of mankind; they spoke of the power of the Resurrection and the indwelling of the Holy Spirit. There was an immediate application: "Christ will provide you with an atmosphere in which you can work out solutions to your problems." Bruce thought, this is the faith. This man is coming very near to showing what it is and where to find it.

On a Tuesday night the message got through in a new and significant way. Bruce was curious to observe the palpitations of his own heart, the irregularity of his breathing. He knew that he had a decision to make. He knew that he would make it. On his way home that night he purchased a Bible at the book table; and on the following Friday at the Cow Palace he walked to the front and went into the counseling room to implement his decision.

> I went forward to accept Christ without any particular emotion except joy in my heart and a feeling that at last

I had found the door to the truth. Immediately things began to happen.

"Billy Graham, of all things!" Fern Warrington fairly snorted when she heard the news. "Why would he go up there?" Actually she knew a lot more about religion than her husband did. She had been exposed early to evangelism of a sort. She had gone to a church youth conference where amid tears she had signed pledges not to smoke or drink, and before leaving high school she had broken both of them. In the years of her married life she had visited a good many churches but had not felt at peace in any of them.

Billy Graham, however, was a new switch, and Fern wanted to know what it was all about. At the invitation of friends she and her younger son, Rich, visited the Cow Palace. As the call was given she went forward even though she was not sure why she was doing it. Bruce heard about it and decided it was typical. She certainly had missed what he had received.

I suddenly found that I had a large number of new friends who had been praying for me and were solidly behind me. The desire for drinking stopped entirely through no effort of my own. I began to sleep better and my mental outlook immediately improved. For several weeks I continued to study and grow in my new Christian life.

Dr. Warrington sent for the Navigators' Bible memory course and began attending his friends' church regularly. On one point, however, he was still adamant: he would not go home. He did not even want to go home. Twenty-three years of hostility could not be cleared up overnight, and no matter how real the Lord had become to him, the basic antagonism remained. As he put it,

A reconciliation with the family still continued to present perplexing problems. This part of the story depended for its solution on the active follow-up work of the Crusade team. I was privileged to attend a week-long conference at Mount Hermon which was led by Associate Evangelists Joseph Blinco and Leighton Ford. . . .

It was no easy task to get away for the Mount Hermon Conference during the first week of July. Scores of patients had to be called and rescheduled, but somehow it was done, and Bruce drove down to the Santa Cruz mountains for a week of inspiration. Someone had given him a copy of Hannah Whitall Smith's classic, *The Christian's Secret of a Happy Life*, and he felt at last that he was moving out spiritually. When he had a word alone with Mr. Blinco, however, he was caught up short: *where was his wife?*

On Thursday Bruce drove back to town and returned with Fern and Rich, the older son being away at camp. That same evening before a packed auditorium at Mount Hermon Bruce gave his first public testimony. He stated that he was aware that his commitment to Jesus Christ was only partial; that he had left out one area that was still unyielded—the area of his family. For Fern it was the first break in the dike, the first clue of hope that something might really happen that would bring their lives together again.

The next day all three Warringtons had a chat with Mr. Blinco. "There must be some concrete, positive expressions of love between you," he said, "but by no means should you start living together until you can pray together." Fern was now facing up to the fact that her first decision had not been real, for she had not yet got to the core of what

138

Christianity was all about. Her remaining questions were, in brief, two: how can God or anyone else love someone like me, and how can I, who think of God usually as only a Punisher, love Him?

Rich, too, was confronted with the greatest challenge of his life. The thirteen-year-old boy had probably been battered by the events of the home more than any other member of the family, yet somehow he had never lost faith that daddy would come back. During the afternoon his mother heard him pacing the room and knew that he was thinking about the evening meeting. Billy Graham had come to spend the day and would be speaking, and giving an invitation.

That night the family sat together in the auditorium and heard the evangelist speak of the forgiveness of the heavenly Father. For Fern it was the crossing of the Rubicon. The cobwebs of fear were brushed away; she saw at last that the love of God in Jesus Christ is even greater than His judgment, and that there is no condemnation for those who trust in Christ as their Savior. At the close Dr. Graham gave his call, and mother and son both responded by going into the prayer room. It was an unforgettable moment. Waiting for Fern was Mr. Blinco, and greeting Rich was young Ed Graham, a cousin of Billy.

On Saturday the Warringtons drove home from Mount Hermon, ostensibly reconciled. Certainly the team and their friends had done what they could. The family had yet to pray together, however. The hate was gone, but still no feeling of closeness prevailed. On Sunday morning Fern developed another of the migraines that have plagued her life, and was unable to accompany her husband to church. Bruce found himself frustrated and as the old feeling of anger returned, in a few moments they realized that they were as far apart as ever.

That evening Bruce lay in bed in his apartment reading Hannah Smith's book. He was in the twelfth chapter and studying these words:

> To the children of God, everything comes directly from their Father's hand, no matter who or what may have been the apparent agents. There are no "second causes" for them. . . . Second causes must all be under the control of our Father, and not one of them can touch us except with His knowledge and by His permission.

Bruce mused over the provocative words. "Everything from God . . . I am to take everything as coming from Him. I am to allow nothing to interfere with His control of my life." He began to see that his married life had been mostly a case of his own interference. That he had never really given this girl a chance. That he had been exasperatingly critical. That his attitudes had produced psychosomatic reactions that had undoubtedly brought on her sicknesses.

Bruce felt humiliated and abased. He called Fern on the telephone and asked her to read chapter twelve in her own copy. Then on the following Tuesday evening he went to the house and sat down with her for a talk. For the first time, it seems, they were able to converse objectively about their differences. Bruce made it clear that he had been given to see his personal responsibility and guilt for the way he had treated her through the years.

They got down on their knees to pray, and the head of the house led them to the throne of Grace. Fern was so overcome that she could not utter a word, but her heart

A total of 623 convicts at San Quentin penitentiary respond to Graham's invitation to decide for Christ.

Service personnel at Treasure Island Naval Station, in the middle of San Francisco Bay, are addressed by Graham.

One of the Crusade's significant meetings: Graham addresses 11,500 students and faculty at the University of California's Greek Theatre.

"Man's moral and spiritual responsibilities" is subject of Graham address before San Francisco's distinguished Commonwealth Club.

Carl Bigelow, Oakland Tribune

Printed banners greet Graham as he speaks to students at
San Francisco State College.

William Crouch, Oakland Tribune

Russ Reed, Oakland Tribune

Over 38,000 people, largest crowd in history of Seals Stadium, fill the home of the San Francisco Giants for the closing rally of the Crusade.

was singing, "Joy! Joy! What I have always wanted! What I have always dreamed . . . !"

We are now building a new life on the solid base of our love for our Lord Jesus Christ. We are taking an active part in a wonderful church near our home, and feel we are approaching a love and understanding which could not have been achieved in any other way.

On Wednesday afternoon, July 9, Bruce Warrington, D.D.S. closed his apartment and moved into his own home.

CHAPTER V · THE RESULTS

Evaluations of the San Francisco Bay Cities Crusade must inevitably reflect the bias of those who make them. Anyone who claims complete objectivity in this field forgets that we are all children of the first Adam, and very human. One of the curious evidences of Billy Graham's mark upon us is the fact that it seems impossible for his contemporaries to be neutral about him. I am pastor of a church that supported the Crusade, and it is from this standpoint that I write.

The proper basis for judging the Crusade is not whether its statistics matched those of New York or London or

Glasgow. In some ways San Francisco outdistanced all the others; in other ways it did not. The real question is whether, in view of the historical background of the area as suggested in the first chapter, such a spiritual Crusade could have any real effect at all.

No one could gather materials for these pages without being impressed with the healthy influence of the Crusade on certain lives. Indeed, to explain what has happened apart from the power of God is to put a high tax on credulity. Nevertheless it has become all too evident in the time since the closing rally that the moral life of the great metropolitan area was barely touched. There was no lessening of the crime rate. The upper strata of San Francisco and peninsula society, with a few exceptions, remained supremely uninterested. There was no outbreak of revival—in the traditional sense—in the churches. It would be a grievous error to claim too much for the work of the Holy Spirit during May and June of 1958. If we are to assess the real values, we must be swayed neither by statistics nor by wishful thinking.

Each time a Billy Graham Crusade comes to a new city, an executive committee of local Christian leaders is formed, and between the committee and the team a set of basic goals is hammered into form. Of necessity the goals vary little from one Crusade to the next. In summary they are: (1) To win as many people as possible in the community to a personal faith in Jesus Christ as Savior and Lord; (2) To encourage and renew the life of the churches; and (3) To bring a new consciousness of God to the surrounding area. Any discussion of the value of the San Francisco Bay Cities Crusade should seek to include these three concerns.

147

1. WINNING NEW CONVERTS

That individuals were genuinely converted to faith in Jesus Christ during the seven weeks of meetings is unquestioned; the stories in this book bear their own evidence. When one asks how many of the 28,254 persons who responded to Billy Graham's invitation either at the Cow Palace or at Seals Stadium were so transformed, he is asking what cannot be disclosed. Only God Himself carries the true statistics of His Kingdom.

As Dr. Graham's work has matured he has shown less interest in its tabulational evidences, and more concern for its spiritual penetration. "I am sick of statistics," he remarked to me one evening at the Cow Palace. Yet the public interest that surrounds his movements requires that some kind of accounting be kept of the results of the meetings. In this sense at least it is true, as one "non-co-operating" minister declared after a friendly interview with the evangelist, that "Billy Graham is a prisoner of his own system."

Each evening the team's press department would post on the Cow Palace press room door the number of people attending, the number of decisions reported and the number of buses parked outside. The newspapers faithfully published the totals; two San Francisco papers, the *Call-Bulletin* and the *News*, actually ran a daily "Graham Box Score" so their readers could check on how Billy was "doing." The figures provided newspaper copy, but they could hardly suggest what was taking place at the Cow Palace.

Human nature being what it is, there were undoubtedly twenty-eight thousand reasons why the twenty-eight thousand people came forward at the San Francisco Crusade. Some came admittedly just "for kicks." Some came out of curiosity to find out what went on in the counseling room.

Some went down because their girl friends or boy friends did, and it was less conspicuous (so it seemed) to go than to remain behind. Some were really confused. Some were Roman Catholic, and went forward as one would go to light a candle in an act of devotion. Some little children went along because they had to accompany their older brothers or sisters. Some adults went forward more than once in order to accompany members of their family. Some were seeking background material for a term paper on religion. Some simply wanted a closer look at Billy Graham. At least one man went forward in an attempt to retain his sanity.

After one has sorted out all the "decisions" that were improperly motivated and were not decisions at all, he finds that they still can have amounted to but a small fraction of the total number of inquirers at the Crusade. To say more is risky, but it seems fair to posit that if a majority—or even a large minority—of the inquirers had come forward for improper reasons the Crusade would never have lasted as long and as successfully as it did. You cannot fool all of the people all of the time. Make due allowance for the margin for error, and it is safe to assume the basic honesty of the work. The New Testament's power does not lie in its statistics, and there is no need for Billy Graham to record one decision for Jesus Christ that is not real.

One of the disturbing post-Crusade revelations to come out of New York was that so many of the people who made decisions in Madison Square Garden never received any communication from any minister, although a return card was mailed to a pastor for each inquirer who came forward. Since the strongest perennial criticism of mass evangelism is that its converts do not last, it is well to have this information. A decision that fails to hold is more than a judgment upon the evangelist, the evangel, or the person involved. It is also a judgment on the Church.

An unbiased sampling of those making decisions in San Francisco would probably reveal that while there are thousands of genuine new Christians in the area, a number have failed to live up to the commitment they made at the Cow Palace. After the way was pointed out to them, they neglected to walk in it. Surely there is nothing new about human frailty. Too often, however, the stumblers are criticized by the wrong people. What would one think of a bachelor who wrote a book criticizing the divorce rate among married people?

San Francisco showed a definite statistical improvement over New York in the proportion of those who maintained spiritual contact after the Crusade. The team reported that in New York only 37 per cent of the cards mailed to ministers were returned; in San Francisco, thanks to a determined effort by the follow-up committee, the figure was over 90 per cent. In New York only 34.5 per cent of the inquirers participated in the Bible study follow-up; in San Francisco the number was at last report 44.6 per cent. Volunteer workers exceeded all previous campaigns; a total of 500 clerical helpers (60 to 80 per night) labored at the Cow Palace during the seven weeks.

After New York it was felt by many that the superlatives were exhausted; the crusade to end crusades had become history, and San Francisco could only be an anticlimax. Before the first week was out, however, it was evident that the first Crusade of the satellite age was breaking new ground.

The team reported not only more counselors trained than in New York but a new level of counseling. Two hundred ministers sat with five thousand laymen through the advance instruction of Lorne Sanny and Charles Riggs. Seven medical doctors were enrolled in a single class. With more advisers available than ever, many of the awkward features of past counseling were eliminated. There were still breakdowns in performance—cards improperly filled out, shortages of personnel on special nights, counselors who forgot their training and told the counselee's story to the adviser instead of letting the inquirer speak for himself, et cetera. In spite of the weaknesses, the work of the counselors stands out as one of the most remarkable aspects of the entire Crusade. To watch people from all walks of life coming forward without pressure, quietly, soberly, reverently, to be joined by unobtrusive friends who were there to help them find what they so earnestly sought, was to recognize that here was a work of sheer *mercy* that was unmatched in the world of our time.

Long after everyone else had left the Cow Palace, a small, picked volunteer staff of laymen and ministers worked each night assigning the decision cards to the designated ministers and churches. The unheralded labors of this crew resulted in the speediest action of any Crusade in getting reports into the hands of the pastors. Here again were some loopholes —not enough liaison with the ministerial committee, improper assignment of some unmarked cards through lack of a thoroughgoing policy, et cetera. Yet the mistakes seem small when measured against the total achievement.

Ushering reached a new peak of efficiency in the Cow Palace, and according to assistant director Bill Brown, San Francisco had more ushers at the start of its campaign than New York had at the end. "These men," he said, "have a depth of purpose; their spirit of co-operation is unusual."

The Cow Palace bar was dismantled and became the ushers' official headquarters.

How does one judge the value of a choir in an evangelistic Crusade? Dwight L. Moody considered his choirs to be of supreme importance, and worked closely with them. Cliff Barrows did not appear on the scene to train his choir for the Cow Palace meetings until a week before they began, but so versatile are his talents and so wide his experience that on the opening afternoon he was able to lead a magnificent chorus of voices in the inspired singing of "How Great Thou Art!"

There are perhaps more opinions in the Church on the subject of music than on any other subject except theology, and Barrows faced an impossible task in trying to please all the Bay Area music lovers. Some quickly got tired of singing the hymn, "Blessed Assurance." Some wished that he would have given his choir something more worthy in the way of anthems. Others would have been content to sing the same songs every night, provided they were familiar. On the nights that the choir rendered Stainer's "Crucifixion" there is no question that the congregation was deeply stirred. When the love of God is combined with great music, heaven seems very close to earth, and no one appears beyond reach of the Holy Spirit.

The loyalty and enthusiasm of the choir was itself a unique development. Massed choirs are not new to San Francisco, but there never was a choir that seemed to love its work as this one. Cliff Barrows' rapport with his singers was obvious from the start. The choir added much to the effectiveness of Dr. Graham's messages, and one of the hardest facts to accept about the ending of the Crusade was the realization that the voice of this great chorus would be stilled.

If human efficiency, ingenuity and quality of performance could have ushered people into the Kingdom of God,
it would have happened in San Francisco. Nothing of the
kind took place, of course. Billy Graham has no secret key
to heaven, and his team has yet to take credit for winning
a soul to Jesus Christ. "How could I ever convert anybody?" cried Graham one night at the Crusade. "This is
God's work." Certainly God keeps the true statistics of
mass evangelism, and they are better left with Him. Whatever portion of the twenty-eight thousand who went forward was born into eternal life is a matter known only to
the Holy Spirit. He is always pleased to use human agencies
when they suit His divine purpose.

2. STRENGTHENING THE CHURCHES

The months that followed the San Francisco Crusade
proved two things conclusively: first, that the participating
churches were abundantly blessed by the meetings, and second, that the blessings did not consist primarily of new ad-
ditions to the rolls. Individual churches felt the effect of
Billy Graham's presence in many ways. At first ministers
were disappointed to find that most of the referral cards
did not provide new timber, but in a number of cases simply
listed their own people. Some were disturbed to find their
loyal and faithful workers suddenly deciding to "accept
Jesus Christ as Savior and Lord." Others were grateful that
it had happened even at that late date.

Most of the decisions of church people were for "re-
affirmation of faith" or "dedication"; and behind many of
these acts of faith there was a vital spiritual history. Gradually the pastors became aware of what was happening: a
process of softening was taking place throughout the congregations. "There is less belligerency among my people,"

declared one astonished shepherd. Even in summertime, larger crowds turned out for prayer meetings and choir practice; new interest was shown in Bible classes; more attention was paid to the pulpit messages; there was better attendance at church suppers, and it was easier to get people to take church jobs. Christianity had become a popular vehicle of conversation, and pastors were heartened to notice the change. Many parishioners had taken the Gospel off the secondhand counter and had made it their own, and were daring to use some of the Church's vocabulary. The simple truth was that the church people had been listening to sermons night after night instead of being diverted by entertainment, and the faith had become a topic of absorbing interest.

Churches that could not point to a single new member resulting from the Crusade meetings could still report a new liveliness among the people in spritual matters. If the churches gave their lay people opportunities to testify, the rewards were stimulating. If a church participated in the visitation evangelism campaign at the conclusion of the Crusade, it found a heart-warming enthusiasm among the callers that made it a worth-while experience, regardless of the numbers added to the roll.

We remain nevertheless a statistics-minded people, and there were pastors and churches in the Bay Area who felt, when it was all over, that there was really not much to report for all the fanfare and activity. Some churches received new members in considerable numbers, but they were the exceptions. Probably the churches that received the greatest lasting benefits were not only those who received the longest lists of referrals, but those whose members were trained as counselors, choir singers and ushers in the Cow Palace, and carried their new-glowing faith back to the home churches.

One of the richest contributions of the Crusade lay in the field of interchurch relations. Wherever Billy Graham has gone, it seems, advances in friendship have taken place between churches and denominational bodies, particularly at the local level. After the Graham team toured the West Indies and Central America in the early months of 1958, George Sanchez of the Navigators visited church leaders in the cities where the meetings had been conducted. Writing in the *Latin America Evangelist*, a periodical published in Costa Rica, he reported:

> One matter constantly reiterated was that never before had there been such a union of effort with so many co-operating. Evangelical groups which heretofore had been satisfied to carry on their own programs fairly exclusively were now anxious and willing to be part of this all-encompassing effort of potent evangelism. Many groups that had never shared the enthusiasm of a common project were drawn together and found themselves working side by side in a real bond of love and oneness in Christ. While we are frank to admit that some of this may subside in time, still there can never be the same lack of interest or even indifference which might have existed between groups prior to the Crusade.

The words could be equally well applied to San Francisco. Before the Bay Cities Crusade began, some evangelicals were disturbed by the circulation of printed literature attacking the Graham team methods, e.g., "Twelve Reasons Why Those Who Obey the Bible Cannot Support the Unscriptural Billy Graham Campaigns." A few local pastors publicly criticized the ecclesiastical support the Crusade was acquiring.

Once the meetings were under way, however, the overwhelming support they received and the enthusiasm they generated seem to have affected the opposition, which subsided. The churches that labored together at the Cow Palace quickly disarmed one another's suspicions, and the walls came tumbling down. Apparent immediately was a bond of unity among evangelicals at the prayer-meeting level. More widely diversified groups began associating congenially at breakfasts and luncheons, and in the activities of choir-singing, counseling and ushering. Even at the theological level there was some regrouping in the days before the Crusade, and by opening day the opinion was more or less crystallized and the positions established. The division was not the one so familiar in America of "liberal" and "evangelical." The great central segment of Protestantism was committed to a mass evangelistic effort as never before. Over 1,100 churches had responded, 200 more than on opening day in New York, and a number of them showed a drive and zeal—not to say hospitality—that astonished the Graham team.

Endorsements came from some councils of churches and denominational offices, although by no means from all. There were friendly expressions from the San Francisco and Oakland Councils of Churches, even though opinion in those councils was divided. Evangelical associations avoided the endorsement issue, but provided much of the local leadership of the Crusade.

An attitude worthy of note was expressed by the Episcopal Diocese of California in a letter urging its clergy and churches to make their own decisions regarding Crusade participation: "We wish Dr. Graham well, feel a sincere friendship, have a sympathetic attitude toward his Gospel message, and pray God's richest blessing upon his endeavor. . . . We urge the prayers of each member of our Communion for him and his forthcoming mission in San Francisco." The Presbytery of San Francisco expressed its approval of the Crusade by majority vote, with some dissent. The headquarters of the Methodist Church had no comment to make, but Methodist churches in general participated more strongly than in New York City, and likewise did the Lutherans. American Baptists and Southern Baptists participated almost to a man, while Pentecostals, Mission Covenanters, Salvation Army, Evangelical Free and independents labored side by side.

San Francisco has always been a melting pot of the races, and it was to be expected that this would be a Crusade in rainbow colors. The Graham team had representatives from England and India as well as an American Negro evangelist. The participation of Negro, Oriental and Spanish-speaking groups in the Crusade was proportionately greater than in New York, and it was a moving sight to witness the interracial counseling at the Cow Palace as black, white, yellow and red led one another into the fullness of the knowledge of Christ.

No official invitation from Bay Area interchurch bodies was ever received by Dr. Graham. An arrangements committee that polled the individual churches found that 397 local congregations desired to have him come, and it was this information that made the team decide in favor of San Francisco. By the time the Crusade opened the number had swelled to 1,188 churches of the region roundabout that had agreed to participate (that is, to join in) or to co-operate (that is, to go along).

How much adjusting and shifting of ground had taken place before the Crusade was evident in the life of the churches after the meetings began. Denominations and local churches which were considered on the theologically liberal side leaned even farther left in an effort to avoid contact with Billy Graham. Within some of the major denominations there was continued opposition to the "techniques of mass evangelism." Similarly some churches which were considered on the far right hardened their views, and were joined by local representatives of ultra-fundamentalist groups across the country who have been increasingly disturbed by Dr. Graham's policy of co-operative evangelism. The kindly, persuasive Christian spirit of Dr. Walter Smyth, Crusade director, and other members of the team seems to have proved a factor in keeping opposition at a minimum.

No statement was issued at any time from the Roman Catholic diocesan office, and the rare comments in the *Monitor*, official organ of the diocese, indicated that the Roman Church sought to treat the Crusade as of minimal importance.

One of the most useful meetings Billy Graham held, from the viewpoint of removing barriers, was with representatives of the many theological seminaries of the Bay Area. Instead of defending his position, he retired from the field with a simple act of faith, pointing out that he was no intellectual, and that his knowledge of theology was probably not so great as many of the students'. The seminarians discovered what everyone else was finding out: that to meet and to hear Billy Graham was to re-evaluate his theology in terms of the man.

It should not be imagined that the Crusade simply created three theological groups—center, left and right—where there had been two before. The traditions and backgrounds of the various seminaries and Bible schools made any such classification impossible, and the religious community's alertness to theological moods and trends meant an inevitable overlapping of positions.

One group that might be distinguished could be called the "evangelical conservatives." These people enjoyed the Crusade greatly, and felt completely at home in the Cow Palace. They provided the heart of the praying and counseling ministry. They came from both the large and small denominations, and night after night they turned out, filling buses with neighbors and friends. Their churches drew the largest number of referrals. Dr. Graham's theology served to strengthen their convictions, while his prophetic message reminded them sharply of their faults, so that many came forward in response to his invitation. Some of the pastors in this group may have had misgivings about the theology of some of Billy's platform guests, but most of them came to join in wholeheartedly as the blessings began to flow.

Perhaps it would be possible also to describe another group as "Graham Admirers." It is a well-known fact that Billy Graham has built up a following among people whose church backgrounds are alien to mass evangelism, but who have been impressed by his mission. These folk may have come from the liturgical churches, the Lutheran, the Episcopal and even the Roman; or they may have come from no church. It would be impossible to group them intellectually or even theologically, beyond a simple statement of faith in Jesus Christ. But there is one thing upon which they were all agreed: they were "for Billy."

Among the opposition, too, there were varying shades of opinion. The extreme right wing has been mentioned; at the other end of the spectrum there were those who could be called "secular liberals," and who opposed Billy Graham on principle. Having little interest in the historic Church to begin with, they looked upon the visiting evan-

gelist as one more ecclesiastical freak, a shouting funda-
mentalist whose ability to win public attention was
something to be endured.

Another group, more difficult to distinguish, might be
considered the "evangelical liberals." These people were
drawn from many backgrounds and shades of churchman-
ship, and because they made up much of the opposition to
the Crusade, they deserve attention. Due to their lack of
sympathy, many of them felt uncomfortable at the Cow
Palace. They likened what occurred there more to a county
fair than to a church service, and felt it was contrary to the
mind and spirit of Jesus. They disliked the "old-time religion" flavor of the meetings and such tools as the King
James Bible and the Gospel song (the one perhaps because
it was too traditional, the other because it was not traditional enough). They suggested that Graham oversimpli-
fied things; that he did not understand the world he lived in,
or the modern-day dilemma of the "man in the gray flan-
nel suit." They considered his doctrine of the Church
inadequate, and they criticized his sermon construction.

A common accusation from this direction was that Graham preached a foreshortened and truncated Gospel. One
seminary professor charged in a letter to the San Francisco
Chronicle that Graham was preaching against the "wrong
sins." Many considered his approach to Scripture ("the
Bible says") as hopelessly outdated and obscurantist; they
felt a man of his stature should be more abreast of new
movements in theology, new discoveries in archaeology and
historical criticism.

Even more, perhaps, they objected to his invitations;
they feared that Graham's emphasis on sin and guilt might
do serious damage to the mental health of his hearers, even
to the producing of mass hysteria. In summary, it could be

said that these sincere church people considered Billy Graham an improvement over Billy Sunday, but they still felt that his Crusades were more interested in exploiting feelings than in producing reverence toward God. For that reason they were glad to see Billy go, so that things could return to normal and (as they would put it) they could get back to the quiet, unostentatious business of following Jesus and seeking to bring in the Kingdom of God.

I have outlined this general position at some length because it highlights the issue that the Crusade presented to a large part of the Christian community in the Bay Area, and makes the success of the Crusade seem even more significant. Before the meetings in the Cow Palace were over, many of these people were to change their minds. They were to weigh the benefits and blessings over against the weaker features, and decide that Billy was on the side of the angels. They were to come to realize that they had been expecting more from Billy than they had a right to expect from any man; that he was doing simply what God had called him to do; that he had no desire to make over twentieth-century Christianity in his own image, but was eager to hear their criticisms in order that he might do his own job better. Once they caught the spirit of the man, and saw the results of his preaching in their midst, a wonderful warming and softening of hearts took place.

The obvious blessing of the Holy Spirit upon Graham's ministry, when studied at first hand, pulled more than one minister off the fence. One surburban pastor spoke for many when he said, "I can't agree with his whole theology, but I can't get over the fact that God is with him." The arrival of decision cards upon pastors' desks; the strong social content of the nightly messages; the courageous facing of community evils; the affectionate relationships among those of diverse social origin, whether on the team, on the executive committee, in the choir, in the counseling room, or in the congregation; and above all the simple proclamation of the Word of God—all of this served to disarm suspicion and win over the reluctant.

At the end of eight weeks the theological center appeared to be more united than it had been in the history of the Far West. There was a noticeable absence of things that have tended to separate Christians. I have suggested that a real secret of Billy Graham's power was his manifest ability to bring believers into touch with one another by omitting the things that divide them. Yet in his final message at Seals Stadium Dr. Graham warned, "Satan would like nothing better than to get us at each other's throats again."

3. BRINGING GOD TO THE COMMUNITY

A profitable subject of research for a graduate student in religion today (providing he could admit his bias) would be an investigation of the effect of a Billy Graham Crusade upon the corporate life of a community. The evangelist has broken new ground in the field, and as yet no real effort has been made to assess it.

In the San Francisco Bay Area the Graham team made a deliberate effort to create a new consciousness of God in the community. Some of it was straight advertising through newspapers, billboards, bumper stickers, et cetera, but the effort went further. It called for an extracurricular ministry on the part of Dr. Graham, and involved a large number of speaking engagements in addition to his nightly stint at the Cow Palace. While members of his team were addressing a wide variety of church groups, Dr. Graham appeared before the San Francisco Commonwealth Club, the Oakland Lake Merritt Breakfast Club, the Rotarians and Kiwanians, the American Red Cross convention, the American Medical Association's Christian wing, businessmen's meetings, theological seminary convocations and other groups. He spoke to two mass meetings, one in San Francisco's Union Square and one in Oakland's City Hall plaza. He visited San Quentin Prison and Folsom Prison with unusual results. Similarly, the local telecast at ten-thirty each night, conducted by Barrows and featuring different speakers, made a tremendous impression on the listening audience, as the three thousand telephone inquiries afterward indicated.

There was no dramatic effort made to invade the domain of the pleasure lovers—no speaking in bars or hotel lobbies, no haranguing of movie crowds. Billy Graham considered a visit to the rendezvous of the "beatniks" in the North Beach area, but decided against it because it would be interpreted by some as a publicity stunt. He agreed reluctantly—after being subpoenaed—to testify at a state legislative hearing on indecent literature. It was quite apparent that the avenues open to the evangelist for reaching the community had their disadvantages.

One channel that did clear was the universities and colleges of the region, and Graham took full advantage of it. He accepted all kinds of limitations on his methods in order to deliver the content of his messages at the University of California, Stanford University and San Francisco State College.

The effect of all these outside messages was to change the attitude of thousands of people completely outside the Church from one of distrust to appreciation. Not only was Billy Graham justified in the eyes of businessmen, students and faculty as a useful citizen, but the Gospel of Jesus Christ was heightened and given new prestige. It is of course one thing to rise in a standing ovation to a gifted evangelist, and another to surrender one's heart to Jesus Christ. Nevertheless seed was sown, misapprehensions were removed and ignorance was replaced with knowledge. Many an organization that was content to believe that "religion is a good thing" was confronted with America's desperate need for a moral and spiritual awakening.

No one would have believed that eleven thousand University of California students would sit attentively and thoughtfully in the Greek Theater—where thousands of eggs have been hurled by underclassmen in past years— to hear an evangelistic message by a man who claimed to be no intellectual. The students were stirred by the sheer moral power of the message and its contrast to the customary academic approach. There was opposition to Billy's coming to the campuses, some of it highly vocal, but the event vindicated itself.

Several weeks after Graham spoke at San Quentin, Chaplain Byron Eshleman reported that fifty men converted at the meeting were continuing a regular course of Bible study. At Folsom Prison Graham was presented with some doggerel signed by the author-inmate and a number of his friends:

> You've said the Lord will clean the slate
>   If we repent before too late,
> That He'd forget bad records made
>   Since we were in the second grade.
> If this is on the level, Billy,
>   Then we won't act so doggone chilly
> When Christ unlocks our prison door
>   And says, "Go forth and sin no more."[1]

[1] As reported in Oakland *Tribune*, July 11, 1958. This visit occurred during a tour of California (including a week at Sacramento) following the San Francisco Crusade.

Perhaps the most accurate gauge to the social penetration of the Bay Cities Crusade was the response of the press. Right from the beginning the news reporters and photographers of the urban dailies had almost an unlimited assignment. They ran galley after galley of type about Billy Graham, his sermons, his personal appearance, his calendar of engagements and his associates, while pictures of the Cow Palace and human interest scenes abounded. "This is way beyond our expectation," said Graham, and the extent of coverage was indeed remarkable for a spiritual event.

The newspapers seemed to take a kind of civic pride in Billy's "Invasion" of the Bay Area. The San Francisco *Call-Bulletin* reprinted the first week's sermons from dictating-machine belts, and mailed Crusade clippings to readers all over the world. The other metropolitan dailies, the *Chronicle*, the *Examiner* and the *News*, likewise considered him front-page news; after the overflow opening, a *Chronicle* reporter admitted, "We are increasing our coverage because the interest of the public seems to warrant it." The most thorough and consistent coverage of the Crusade was provided by the Rev. Mr. Rose in the Oakland *Tribune*. Rose was assigned full-time to the Crusade and proved a gifted interpreter of Graham's messages.

Radio and television outlets in the Bay Area also served to bring the Crusade to the attention of the public, and the response to the team personalities was highly favorable. When we press further, however, and ask what the response was to the *message* of the Crusade, we find a curious silence. Even the newspapers which were so generous in their coverage, failed to undertake any kind of thoughtful appraisal of the Graham mission, either through the columnists or in the editorial columns. Thus the mass media were most co-operative in enabling the Crusade to reach the man in the street, but—perhaps because of a desire to be objective or owing to a sensitivity to all religious issues —failed to speak for the community. It remained for the mayors of San Francisco and Oakland, George Christopher and Clifford Rishell, to state in positive and forthright terms before the vast Crusade crowds, the appreciation and commendation of the populace for the presence of the Graham team, and to declare, "We are a better people because you have been here."

It will take four years, in the estimation of the team, for the full results of the San Francisco Bay Cities Crusade to be known. The young men converted in the London Crusade of 1954 only began coming into the ministry of the Gospel in Great Britain in 1958.

Meanwhile the City by the Golden Gate that "has lived a thousand lives in its hundred years, and is still fresh and buoyant as the ocean breezes" moves along about the same —or does it? Surely it is too much to say that the city is now conscious of God; San Francisco has never been fully conscious of God. Yet as one reflects on the great days of the faith in the west—when Christians "lost their inferiority complex," as one reporter put it—when great music pealed from the Cow Palace, and a strong young voice pointed to sin and to the Cross, when the masses heard the Word proclaimed, and some came back at midnight to pound on locked doors and cry for help—when strong men wept and little children leaped for joy—when habits were broken, cold hearts were melted and homes were restored— one can say that in a real sense San Francisco will never be quite the same.

CHAPTER VI · THE MESSAGE

KEYNOTE SERMON PREACHED BY BILLY GRAHAM
IN THE COW PALACE, SUNDAY AFTERNOON,
APRIL 27, 1958[1]

We are delighted with the tremendous reception we have received in this area, and with the demonstration this afternoon which in my opinion is indicative of a spiritual hunger on the part of millions of Americans at this most critical hour of our history.

We have come here this afternoon, not under the sponsorship, not under the direction of the churches or the executive committee or the Billy Graham team or any other organization. We have come here sponsored and directed

[1] As reported in the San Francisco *Call-Bulletin* and other newspapers.

we believe by the Holy Spirit. And we have come here to exalt Jesus Christ as Savior and Lord and Master.

We have not come here to put on a show. We have not come here to entertain you in the Cow Palace. We have come here to open this ancient book called the Holy Bible. We are going to open the pages of the Bible night after night and see what this Book has to say. We've heard the voice of the diplomats. We've heard the voice of the scientists. We've heard the voice of the psychiatrists. We've heard the voice of the sociologists. We've heard the voice of our military commanders. Now I believe that it's time we listen to the voice of Almighty God. And I believe that within the pages of this Book there is an answer to the problems that we face as a world and as a nation, and the problems you face as an individual. And so night after night it will be my privilege to open this Book and explain to you what the Bible says—in the language of the people. I'm going to use the language that the people on the street use in trying to explain to you what the Bible says and I'm going to try to make it so simple that even the children can understand it.

Almost everybody today has a Bible. You own a Bible, you have one in your home; but very few of us are reading the Bible and very few know what the Bible has to say. So night after night we are going to open the Bible and see what the Bible has to say. Therefore, I'm going to ask all of you to bring your Bibles tomorrow night.

I want you to turn with me for our message today to the first chapter of Isaiah the prophet, first verse:

> The vision of Isaiah the son of Amoz, which he saw concerning Judah and Jerusalem in the days of Uzziah, Jotham, Ahaz, and Hezekiah, kings of Judah. Hear, O

heavens, and give ear, O earth: for the Lord hath spoken, I have nourished and brought up children, and they have rebelled against me. The ox knoweth his owner, and the ass his master's crib: but Israel doth not know, my people doth not consider. Ah sinful nation, a people laden with iniquity, a seed of evildoers, children that are corrupters: they have forsaken the Lord, they have provoked the Holy One of Israel unto anger, they are gone away backward. Why should ye be stricken any more? Ye will revolt more and more: the whole head is sick, and the whole heart faint. From the sole of the foot even unto the head there is no soundness in it; but wounds, and bruises, and putrefying sores: they have not been closed, neither bound up, neither mollified with ointment. Your country is desolate, your cities burned with fire: your land, strangers devour it in your presence, and it is desolate, as overthrown by strangers. And the daughter of Zion is left as a cottage in a vineyard, as a lodge in a garden of cucumbers, as a besieged city.

Except the Lord of hosts had left unto us a very small remnant, we should have been as Sodom, and we should have been like unto Gomorrah.

Hear the word of the Lord, ye rulers of Sodom; give ear unto the law of our God, ye people of Gomorrah. To what purpose is the multitude of your sacrifices unto me? saith the Lord: I am full of the burnt offerings of rams, and the fat of fed beasts; and I delight not in the blood of bullocks, or of lambs, or of he goats. When ye come to appear before me, who hath required this at your hand, to tread my courts? Bring no more vain oblations; incense is an abomination unto me; the new moons and sabbaths, the calling of assemblies, I cannot away with; it is iniquity, even the solemn meeting. Your new moons and your appointed feasts my soul hateth: they are a trouble unto me; I am weary to bear them. And when ye spread forth your hands, I will hide mine eyes from you: yea, when ye make many prayers, I will not hear: your hands are full of blood.

Wash you, make you clean; put away the evil of your doings from before mine eyes; cease to do evil; learn to do well; seek judgment, relieve the oppressed, judge the fatherless, plead for the widow. Come now, and let us reason together, saith the Lord: though your sins be as scarlet, they shall be as white as snow; though they be red like crimson, they shall be as wool. If ye be willing and obedient, ye shall eat the good of the land: but if ye refuse and rebel, ye shall be devoured with the sword: for the mouth of the Lord hath spoken it.

Eight hundred years before Christ that was written with the prophetic eye and the prophetic pen of Isaiah the prophet. God had already sent His kings and His judges to Judah and to Israel. And now He is speaking through His prophet and He says, "Ye are a sinful people," and He says, "Unless you repent of your sins ye shall be destroyed." He does not say whether some other nation is going to come and destroy them or whether they are going to come under the fiery judgment of God Himself. But God warns the people that unless there is national repentance there is going to be judgment.

I want to speak this afternoon on four points: first, the mounting confusion; second, the frantic quest; third, the proper diagnosis, and fourth, the needed encounter.

1

We are living in a day of mounting confusion. All over the world men's hearts are failing them because of fear. The arms race is gathering tremendous momentum. Many of our world problems such as the Middle East have only been patched up. They have not been permanently solved and can break out at any moment in a terrible holocaust that could send the world into a flaming war and destroy civilization.

We are facing economic troubles today. Did you know that the population of India is increasing at the rate of 5,000,000 a year? Five million new mouths to feed every year in India which cannot even keep up with the expansion of the five-year program! Did you know that Japan has a land area less than the size of the state of California and 93,000,000 people live in Japan? Suppose 93,000,000 people lived in California, increasing at the rate of 1,000,000 a year. That alone is going to bring about economic pressures around the world that could touch off war at any time.

We are facing technological problems. Man is expanding farther and farther and faster and faster. And we are told that we may get to the moon this year. And it is predicted that within ten years we will fly from New York to London in one hour by rocket ship. And yet Bertrand Russell, the great philosopher, looking at all these technological advances, says that he wouldn't give a fifty-fifty chance that there'll be one human being left on this planet forty years from now. And an American scientist answering him said, "I would not give you a fifty-fifty chance that there will be one human being left on this planet *twenty* years from now."

Our racial problems are not confined to a certain part of the United States but are world-wide. The great problem in the Middle East is racial. The great problems of India are basically racial. And the racial tension in many parts of the world is rising. We have moral problems! In business, in labor and in government we are seeing one scandal after another. Dishonesty, lying, cheating, greed, lust, on every side. We have taught during the last generation that morality is relative rather than absolute and now we are reaping the results in dishonesty, lying, cover-up and hypocrisy.

And our teen-agers—what shall I say about many of them? In this morning's paper it said that the situation in New York has become critical among teen-agers. All over the country there is teen-age crime. This past year most of the major crimes in the United States were committed by teen-agers. We've taken God and the Bible out of our schools and now we are reaping the whirlwind of the wind that we have sown. And now education is in a crisis. And a Chicago judge said the other day the teen-age criminals today make Al Capone's gang look like a Sunday School class.

Our generation is filled with nervous tension. There is a revolt against all restraint, and a terrible gnawing fear on the part of everybody. We are enjoying the greatest prosperity in the history of the world and at the same time we are more nervous than any generation of people. Almost every businessman who is a success has an ulcer. And we are taking tranquilizing pills by the million, sleeping pills to put us to sleep at night, dexedrine tablets to wake us up in the morning and aspirins thrown in between. No wonder Sir Winston Churchill recently said, "Our problems are beyond us."

A foreign correspondent for one of our big city newspapers said recently, "We are living in a night of total crisis, and the fellowship of fear is universal." A news magazine had as a headline the other day, "The whole world in trouble." And all over the world instead of our problems getting better, they are getting worse. Year by year it is worse than it was the year before.

2

We've lost our spiritual sensibilities. We've lost our contact with the supernatural—with the Harmonizer and Co-ordinator of the universe. A European leader said about a year ago, "If the devil offers a solution to the problems of the world, I will gladly follow the devil." The whole world is frantically, madly searching for an answer before we blow ourselves to bits.

Let me tell you something—the philosophers, the scientists, the political leaders and intellectuals are beginning to say, "We need God!" For the first time in modern history even the scientist is saying that we need God. There is an admission that we have lost God somewhere. Our generation needs God more than any generation in the history of the world. Look at the individuals around you—people that you think should be happy—miserable. We are beginning to find that glamor and money and a high standard of living do not bring happiness and joy to the soul. There must be something else in life. There must be something out there somewhere. What is it?

There is a new word that has entered our vocabularies —"escapism." We Americans are trying to escape from reality and therefore we are going to dope; and here in San Francisco, as well as all over the world, hundreds are turning to drink and entertainment. We have to have entertainment every moment. Between aspirin tablets we switch our television channels and if the TV isn't on, we have the radio blaring or some magazine in our hands. It seems that if a man has a million dollars and if a person is at the top of the social ladder, or if a person is a film star or a television star, they ought to be happy. It seems that if you have a home and a family out here in California, you ought to be happy

—but you're not. What's wrong? You're out of balance. There's something wrong! What is it? You can't find the answer. One man said to me, "I'd give a million dollars to be happy." I said, "You can't buy happiness." He said, "I know it." What's wrong?

3

This Book tells us. The Bible teaches that you have a body with eyes, ears, nose, tongue, hands, feet . . . but down inside your body is something else. You are a living soul, created in the image of God. Deep down inside of you is a soul. When I look at you, I don't see you. I see the house you live in. When I show you my watch, you don't actually see my watch. You only see the case that the watch lives in. Deep down inside of you is your soul, made in the image of God.

Now, this questing, this searching, this looking for something outside of yourself to bring peace and joy and happiness is your soul. You can't satisfy your soul by getting drunk. You can't satisfy the longing of your soul by a sex experience. You can't satisfy your soul by gambling. You can't satisfy your soul by entertainment.

The Bible teaches, "For all—all—A-L-L—have sinned"; whatever your social standing, whatever your financial accounting, whatever your racial background; whoever you are, "For ALL have sinned and come short of the glory of God." That's your trouble. That's my trouble. We are sinners. You say, "Now wait a minute, Billy. You can say all of that in New York; we know they're sinners back there. But this is the Bay Area, and we're not so bad out here." The Bible says that the best of you have sinned against God.

Do you know what sin is? Sin is the breaking of the Ten

Commandments. It is the transgression of the Law. And every person in this audience today has broken the Ten Commandments. But suppose you had kept all the commandments and had only broken one: the Bible says you are guilty of all. But in addition to that, sin means that you have come short of God's moral requirements. We have failed to live up to the Sermon on the Mount. We have failed to live up to the teachings of Christ. We have all sinned. We have failed. The Bible says that God, being a Holy God, cannot look on sin. And so we find ourselves separated from God by sin.

4

Now God loves us. God wants to help us. But God can do nothing for us until we come to Him. The Bible says that sin brings about judgment. The Bible says, "God judgeth the righteous, and God is angry with the wicked" (Ps. 7:11). And the Bible says that Jesus said (I didn't), "Except ye repent, ye shall all likewise perish" (Luke 13:3). The Bible again says, "For the wrath of God is revealed from heaven against all ungodliness and unrighteousness of men, who hold the truth in unrighteousness" (Rom. 1:18). The Bible teaches that God is going to judge sin; and we are sinners. We are under the judgment of God.

You cannot make a better world until you've made better men. Oh, I know that if the whole world should suddenly become Christian, it wouldn't solve every problem. I know that, because you can take a Christian family and they still have their tensions. But if the whole world should turn to Christ, if the whole world were converted, it would create an atmosphere in which problems could be solved. Christ would reign supreme. He would be the Lord.

What is conversion? Many people have an idea that

it is some emotional experience that a person has, and you either get it or you don't get it. It's not that at all. Jesus said, "Except a man be born again, he cannot see the kingdom of God" (John 3:3). Whether you understand or not, you give yourself to Christ by faith. And when should this encounter take place? The Bible says, "Now is the accepted time; behold, now is the day of salvation" (II Cor. 6:2).

It is a dangerous thing to hear the message and to do nothing about it. This is your moment with God; it may never come again just like this. You need Christ. You need to come to the Cross. You need the courage and strength God can give you. I am inviting you to do something about it now. I am inviting you to come forward and give your heart to Jesus Christ. You come.